Busy Ant Maths

Pupil Book 4C

Series Editor: Peter Clarke

Authors: Elizabeth Jurgensen, Jeanette Mumford, Sandra Roberts

Contents

Unit 9 — Page number

Week 1: Number – Number and place value
- Lesson 1: Get in order — 4
- Lesson 2: Rounding to the nearest 10, 100 or 1000 — 5
- Lesson 3: Negative numbers (2) — 6
- Lesson 4: Roman numerals — 7

Week 2: Number – Addition and subtraction, incl. Measurement (money)
- Lesson 1: Written addition (5) — 8
- Lesson 2: Written subtraction (5) — 9
- Lesson 3: How many teeth? — 10
- Lesson 4: Ordering and adding money — 11

Week 3: Geometry – Properties of shape
- Lesson 1: All sorts of triangles — 12
- Lesson 2: Parallelogram and rhombus — 13
- Lesson 3: Trapezium and kite — 14
- Lesson 4: Know your quadrilaterals — 15

Unit 10

Week 1: Number – Multiplication and division
- Lesson 1: Multiplication HTO × O using the formal written method (1) — 16
- Lesson 2: Multiplication HTO × O using the formal written method (2) — 17
- Lesson 3: Multiplication HTO × O using the most efficient method — 18
- Lesson 4: Solving word problems (3) — 19

Week 2: Number – Fractions
- Lesson 1: Equivalent fractions (3) — 20
- Lesson 2: Adding fractions — 21
- Lesson 3: Subtracting fractions — 22
- Lesson 4: Table fractions — 23

Week 3: Measurement (volume and capacity)
- Lesson 1: Filling station litres — 24
- Lesson 2: Science lab litres — 25
- Lesson 3: Estimating and rounding capacity — 26
- Lesson 4: Litres of juice — 27

Unit 11	Page number

Week 1: Number – Addition and subtraction, incl. Measurement (money)
- Lesson 1: Meet the target (1) — 28
- Lesson 2: Meet the target (2) — 29
- Lesson 3: Ordering and subtracting money — 30
- Lesson 4: Lunch problems — 31

Week 2: Number – Decimals
- Lesson 1: Decimal tenths and hundredths — 32
- Lesson 2: Comparing and rounding decimals — 33
- Lesson 3: Dividing by 10 and 100 — 34
- Lesson 4: Decimal problems — 35

Week 3: Geometry – Position and direction
- Lesson 1: Take off coordinates — 36
- Lesson 2: Constellation coordinates — 37
- Lesson 3: Coordinates of shapes — 38
- Lesson 4: Plotting points and making shapes — 39

Unit 12

Week 1: Number – Multiplication and division
- Lesson 1: Division TO ÷ O using partitioning — 40
- Lesson 2: Division TO ÷ O using the formal written method — 41
- Lesson 3: Division HTO ÷ O using partitioning — 42
- Lesson 4: Division using the expanded written method — 43

Week 2: Number – Multiplication and division
- Lesson 1: Division using the formal written method (1) — 44
- Lesson 2: Division using the formal written method (2) — 45
- Lesson 3: Division using the most efficient method — 46
- Lesson 4: Solving word problems (4) — 47

Week 3: Statistics
- Lesson 1: Dice bar charts — 48
- Lesson 2: Harbour times — 50
- Lesson 3: Activity Centre data — 52
- Lesson 4: Travel time graphs — 54

Maths facts — 56

Unit 9, Week 1, Lesson 1

Get in order

Order and compare numbers beyond 1000

Challenge 1

Order each set of numbers, smallest to largest.

a 3762, 7645, 2651, 8625, 4488
b 7628, 5037, 7282, 5119, 7481
c 6387, 6182, 6064, 6339, 6292
d 7612, 8632, 7688, 6522, 8011
e 8373, 9373, 7393, 8363, 7383
f 2766, 2812, 2934, 2048, 2533
g 7129, 3827, 3277, 2981, 7035
h 5487, 5981, 5328, 5310, 5387

Challenge 2

Work in fours.

- Each player has two pieces of paper. Everyone secretly writes a 4-digit number on each of their pieces of paper.
- One player takes all the papers, and without looking at the numbers, shuffles them and puts them in a pile face down on the table.
- All players write the numbers 1 to 8 as a list in their books. At the top of the page, write 'largest' and at the bottom write 'smallest'.
- Players take it in turns to turn over the top paper and decide where to write the number on their list.
- If you cannot write a number in order, write it on the side.

You will need:
- eight small pieces of paper

Remember you want to try and get all the numbers in order.
How many numbers did you get in order?

Challenge 3

Copy out these numbers and write a number in the spaces, still keeping the order.

a 2675, ____, 3871, ____, ____, 4877, ____, ____, 4952
b 3000, ____, ____, 3100, ____, 3200, ____, ____, 3259
c ____, 4762, ____, 4892, ____, ____, 4999, ____, 5010
d ____, 5198, ____, ____, 5500, ____, 5550, ____, 5560
e 6899, ____, ____, 6976, ____, 7000, ____, ____, 7100
f 4010, ____, 4020, ____, ____, ____, 4030, ____, 4050
g ____, 8455, ____, ____, 8480, ____, 8501, ____, 8520
h 9078, ____, ____, 9150, ____, 9345, ____, ____, 9455

Unit 9, Week 1, Lesson 2

Rounding to the nearest 10, 100 or 1000

Round any number to the nearest 10, 100 or 1000

Challenge 1

1. Write the two multiples of 10 that each number comes between on either side of the number.

   > **Example**
   > 1230 ← 1236 → (1240)

   a 614   b 789   c 865   d 1362
   e 1718   f 2064   g 2637   h 3525

2. Circle the multiple of 10 that the number rounds to.

Challenge 2

1. Write the two multiples of 100 that each number comes between on either side of the number.

   a 2189   b 3577   c 6252   d 7808   e 9458

2. Now look at the 10s digit and decide whether the number should be rounded up or down. Circle the correct multiple of 100.

3. Write the two multiples of a 1000 that each number comes between on either side of the number.

   > **Example**
   > 4000 ← 4628 → (5000)

   a 2768   b 3289   c 4890   d 4178   e 5098
   f 5318   g 6588   h 6982   i 7437   j 9534

4. Circle the multiple of 1000 that the number rounds to.

Challenge 3

1. Write the multiples of 100 and 1000 that each number comes between, on either side of the number.

   > **Example**
   > (3700)   3800
   >   ↖ 3725 ↗
   > 3000   (4000)

   a 4572   b 4138   c 5269   d 4731
   e 5934   f 6495   g 7065   h 8472

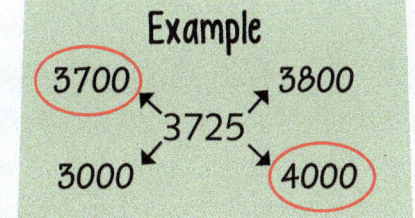

2. Circle the multiples of 100 and 1000 that the number rounds to.

3. Explain the rules for rounding numbers to the nearest 1000.

Unit 9, Week 1, Lesson 3

Negative numbers (2)

Count backwards through 0 to include negative numbers

Challenge 1

Start at these numbers and count back 5. Record your numbers on a number line.

a −5   b −8   c −13

d −26   e −31   f −37

Example

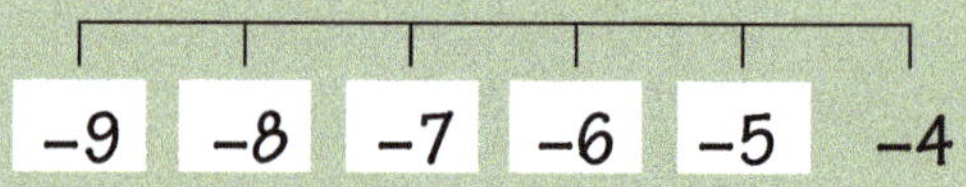

| −9 | −8 | −7 | −6 | −5 | −4 |

Challenge 2

1 What is 8 less than:

a −4   b −7   c −12   d −33   e −24   f −30

2 What is 11 less than:

a −9   b −26   c −35   d −41   e −24   f −45

3 Look at the two temperatures. How much have they changed by?

a 7 degrees to −5 degrees

b 3 degrees to −8 degrees

c −3 degrees to −15 degrees

d −3 degrees to 12 degrees

Challenge 3

1 Look at these temperatures.

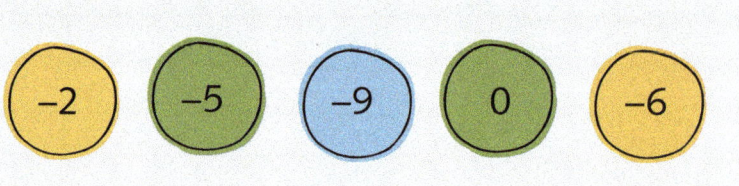

−2   −5   −9   0   −6

a For each one, what would the temperature be if the weather got warmer by 7 degrees?

b What would the temperature be if the weather got colder by 13 degrees?

2 Write five word problems about changes of temperature, involving negative numbers. Make sure you have worked out the answers. Swap your problems with a partner.

Unit 9, Week 1, Lesson 4

Roman numerals

Read and write Roman numerals to 100

Hint
Five important Roman numerals to remember:
I = 1
V = 5
X = 10
L = 50
C = 100

Challenge 1

1 Write the numbers 1 to 20 in Roman numerals.

2 Write the next Roman numeral after each of these.

　a V　　b VII　　c III　　d IV　　e VI
　f X　　g XV　　h XII　　i XVI　　j XIV

Challenge 2

1 Write the numbers 20 to 50 in Roman numerals.

2 Write the next Roman numeral after each of these.

　a XVI　　b XXV　　c XXVII　　d XXIX　　e XXXIII
　f XXXV　　g XL　　h XLII　　i XLV　　j L

3 Work with a partner. Write these Roman numerals on small pieces of paper.

You will need:
- eight small pieces of paper

Example
40 = XL

I I I V X X X L

Take turns to say a number between 1 and 50. Use the cards to make that Roman numeral.

Challenge 3

1 Write the numbers 50 to 100 in Roman numerals.

2 Do you think the Roman numeral system is a good one or not? Why?

3 Investigate the times tables in Roman numerals. Are there any times tables answers that make a pattern? Explain any patterns that you notice.

Example
I × V = V
II × V = X
III × V = XV
IV × V =

Unit 9, Week 2, Lesson 1

Written addition (5)

- Add numbers with up to 4 digits using the formal written method of columnar addition
- Estimate and use inverse operations to check answers to a calculation

Challenge 1

1 Estimate the answers to these calculations and then work them out.

   a 568 + 317   b 492 + 365   c 1264 + 1383
   d 1469 + 1218   e 1426 + 1832   f 1372 + 1451

2 Estimate the answers to these calculations and then work them out.

   a 643 + 269   b 548 + 394   c 1527 + 2615
   d 1364 + 2277   e 2906 + 1356   f 2364 + 1807

Challenge 2

1 Estimate the answers to these calculations and then work them out.

   a 2867 + 1354   b 3827 + 2376   c 3716 + 2495
   d 4386 + 3824   e 5294 + 2817   f 6528 + 2694

2 Estimate the answers to these calculations and then work them out. Think carefully about how you lay them out.

   a 3854 + 326   b 2384 + 548   c 3072 + 943
   d 4575 + 819   e 5836 + 784   f 6532 + 849

3 Check your calculations using the inverse operation.

Challenge 3

1 Estimate the answers to these calculations and then work them out.

   a 5718 + 544   b 5006 + 799   c 6761 + 853   d 5873 + 578
   e 4999 + 604   f 5782 + 459   g 5998 + 699   h 7397 + 764

2 Check your calculations using the inverse operation.

3 Which of the calculations in Question 1 could you work out more efficiently mentally?

8

Unit 9, Week 2, Lesson 2

Written subtraction (5)

- Subtract numbers with up to 4 digits using the formal written method of columnar subtraction
- Estimate and use inverse operations to check answers to a calculation

Challenge 1

Work out these calculations using the written method.
Think carefully about how you lay them out.

a 2653 – 371   b 2175 – 631   c 2836 – 728   d 3925 – 684
e 3555 – 722   f 3721 – 714   g 4265 – 613   h 4276 – 835

Challenge 2

1 Estimate the answers to these calculations and then work them out.

a 4387 – 648   b 4282 – 756   c 5361 – 846   d 5952 – 841
e 6735 – 758   f 6553 – 875   g 7344 – 866   h 7683 – 795

2 Check your calculations using the inverse operation.

3 These 9 numbers can be used to make 3 subtraction calculations, including their answers. Can you work out what the calculations are?

3468   295   4905   379   3748   2987   4043   481   4526

Challenge 3

1 Estimate the answers to these calculations.

a 7452 – 877   b 8473 – 685   c 8333 – 888
d 9637 – 869   e 9326 – 549   f 9175 – 486

2 Check your calculations using the inverse operation.

3 Can these calculations be done easily using the written method? Explain the reasons for your answer.

a 7004 – 872   b 5008 – 461   c 4000 – 299

Unit 9, Week 2, Lesson 3

How many teeth?

Solve problems in contexts, deciding which operations and methods to use and why

How many teeth are there in your school?

Challenge 1

Find out how many teeth in your class.

Questions to help you:

- How many children in your class?
- How many adults in your class?

Most children have 20 teeth and most adults have 32 teeth.

Challenges 2, 3

Find out approximately how many teeth in your school.

Questions to help you:

- How many children are there in each year group?
- How many adults are there in your school?

Be sure to show all your working and explain your reasoning.

- How accurate do you think your answer is? Explain why.

Do you need to count everyone's teeth?

Challenge 3

When the school dentist comes, she says she only has time to see 2000 teeth. The Head says adults get their teeth checked first. How many children will the dentist be able to check?
Be sure to show all your working and explain your reasoning.

10

Unit 9, Week 2, Lesson 4

Ordering and adding money

Estimate, compare and calculate with money in euros and cents

Challenge 1

1. Order these amounts of money, smallest to largest.
   - a €5.80, €8.50, €5.05, €8.08, €5.50, €5.15
   - b €12.34, €13.42, €13.20, €12.40, €12.04, €13.04

2. Add these amounts of money mentally.
   - a €35.10 + €2.40
   - b €28.50 + €14.30
   - c €41.70 + €35.00

3. Add these amounts of money using the formal written method.
   - a €43.25 + €21.32
   - b €57.28 + €35.51
   - c €46.38 + €47.61

Challenge 2

1. Order these amounts of money, smallest to largest.
   - a €54.39, €54.00, €45.99, €45.10, €54.93, €45.07
   - b €94.51, €94.15, €94.01, €94.00, €94.05, €94.55

2. Add these amounts of money mentally.
   - a €67.90 + €47.80
   - b €79.65 + €38.00
   - c €124.50 + €68.10

3. Add these amounts of money using the formal written method.
   - a €87.75 + €45.18
   - b €96.35 + €62.87
   - c €285.65 + €173.72

Challenge 3

1. Using these digits make ten different amounts of money. Remember, they all need to be €HTO.th, such as €759.68.

   5   6   7   8   9

2. Write your amounts in order, smallest to largest.
3. Using your amounts write eight addition calculations to work out.

Unit 9, Week 3, Lesson 1

All sorts of triangles

Use properties and sizes to compare and classify triangles

Challenges 1, 2

Measure the sides of each triangle. Copy and complete the table by writing the letter of each triangle in the correct place.

You will need:
- ruler

Equilateral Three sides equal	
Isosceles Two sides equal	
Scalene No sides equal	

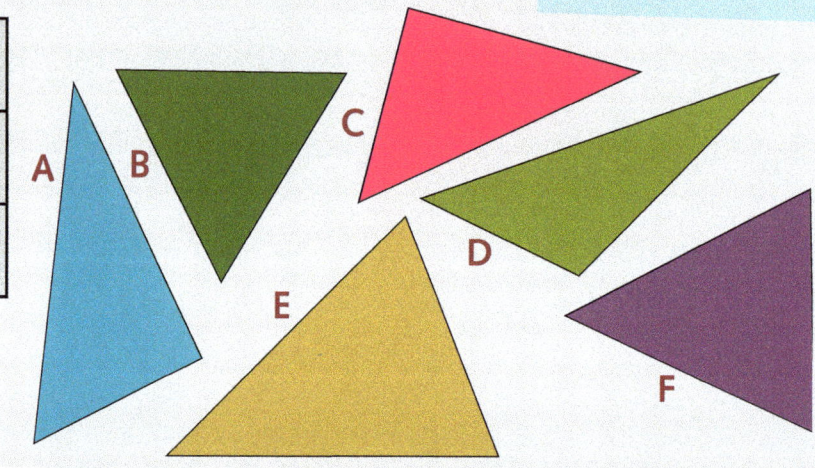

Challenge 2

1 Copy these right angles on to squared paper.

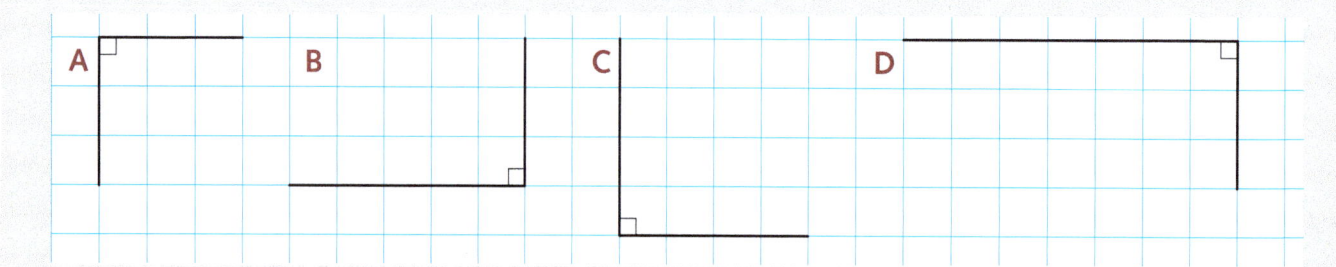

2 Draw one more line to make a right-angled triangle.

3 Write the letters of the triangles which are right-angled and then the letters of the triangles that are isosceles.

You will need:
- squared paper
- ruler

Challenge 3

How many different isosceles triangles can you find in a regular pentagon? Investigate.

Use Resource 54: Pentagons. For each pentagon:

a draw the diagonals with your ruler

b find an isosceles triangle and colour it in

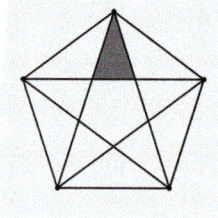

You will need:
- Resource 54: Pentagons
- ruler
- coloured pencil

Unit 9, Week 3, Lesson 2

Parallelogram and rhombus

Use properties and sizes to compare and classify parallelograms and rhombuses

Challenge 1

Copy and complete the table, putting the letter of each shape in the correct column.

You will need:
- ruler

Square	Rectangle	Rhombus	Parallelogram
	A,		

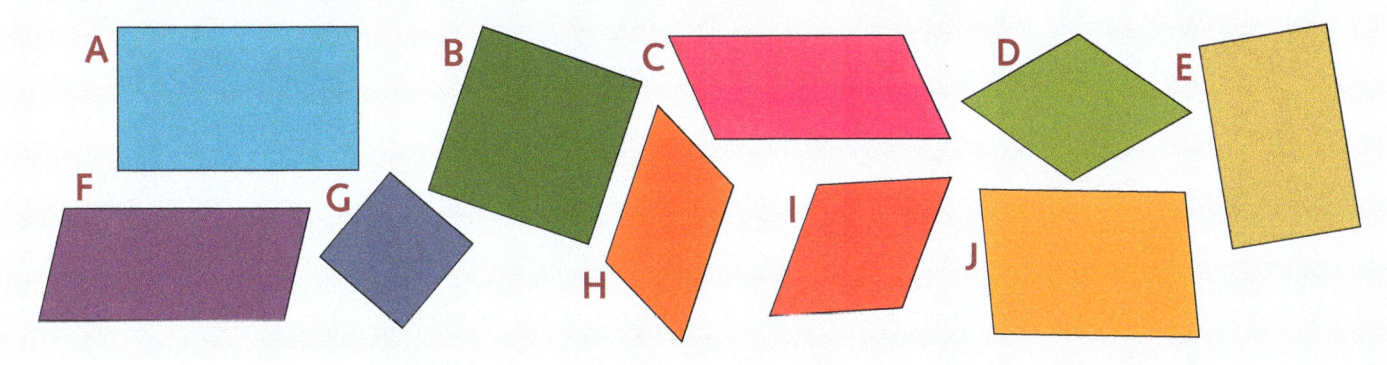

Challenge 2

Copy and complete the table. Write ✓ for yes and ✗ for no.

Quadrilateral	Opposite sides equal	Opposite sides parallel	Opposite angles equal	All sides equal	Four right angles
Square					
Rectangle					
Parallelogram					
Rhombus					

Challenge 3

1. Copy these quadrilaterals on to 1 cm square dot paper.

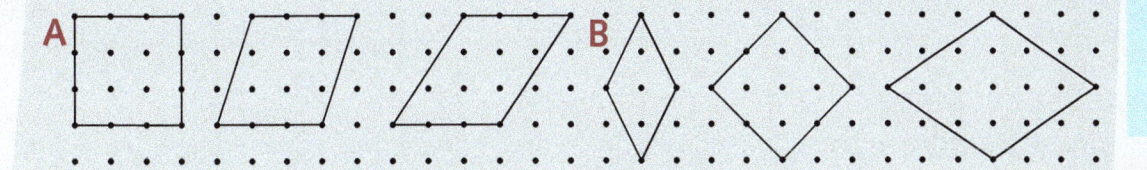

You will need:
- 1 cm square dot paper
- ruler

2. Draw the next two shapes in each sequence.

3. Check each sequence of five quadrilaterals for line symmetry. Write what you notice.

Unit 9, Week 3, Lesson 3

Trapezium and kite

Use properties and sizes to compare and classify trapeziums and kites

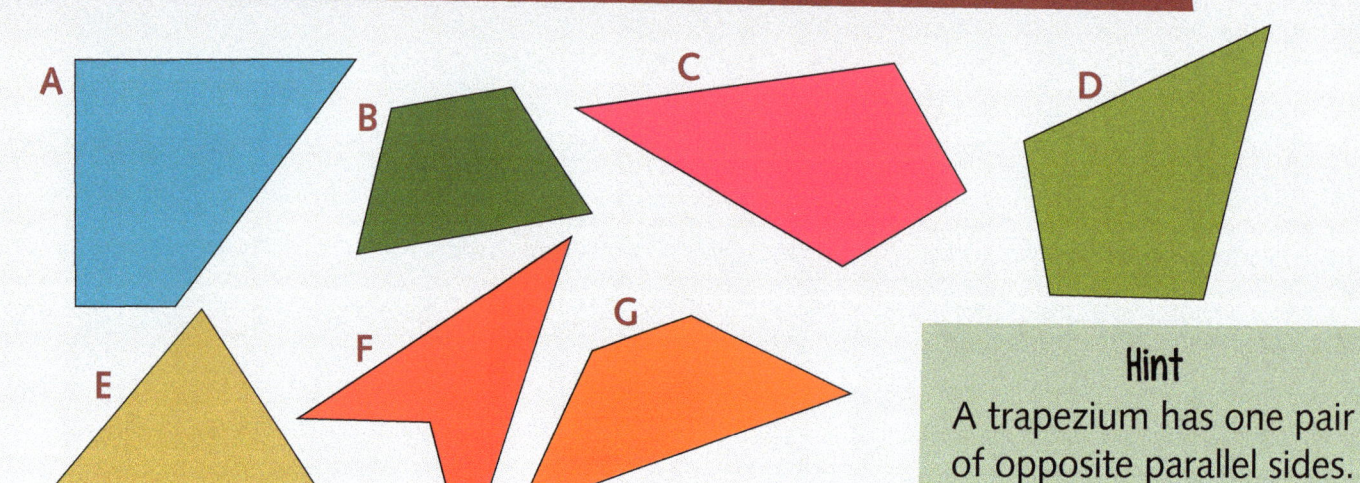

Hint
A trapezium has one pair of opposite parallel sides.

A kite has two pairs of adjacent sides equal.

Challenges 1, 2

1. Name shapes A to G.
2. On 1 cm square dot paper draw:
   a. three different trapeziums
   b. three different kites

You will need:
- 1 cm square dot paper
- ruler
- right-angle tester

Challenge 2

Write the letters of the shapes at the top of the page which have:

a. only one pair of opposite parallel sides

b. two pairs of adjacent sides equal

c. one line of symmetry

d. one or more right angles

e. two acute and two obtuse angles

Challenge 3

1. Use Resource 54: Pentagons. For four pentagons, draw the diagonals with a ruler.
2. Use your four pentagons to find and record in colour:
   a. two different trapeziums   b. two different kites

You will need:
- Resource 54: Pentagons
- ruler
- coloured pencils

Unit 9, Week 3, Lesson 4

Know your quadrilaterals

Use properties and sizes to compare and classify quadrilaterals

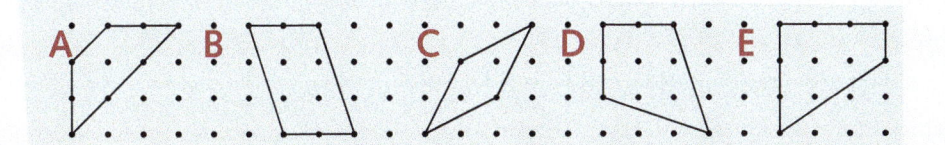

You will need:
- 1 cm square dot paper
- ruler
- coloured pencils

1. Write the name of each quadrilateral.

2. Copy the quadrilaterals on to 1 cm square dot paper.

   For each quadrilateral mark:

   a the equal sides

   b each pair of equal angles in a different colour

Copy and complete the table for each of the above quadrilaterals. Write ✓ for yes and ✗ for no.

Properties	A	B	C	D	E
One or more lines of symmetry					
Opposite sides equal					
Adjacent sides equal					
At least one pair of opposite sides parallel					
Opposite angles equal					
At least one pair of perpendicular sides					

Write two ways in which these pairs of quadrilaterals are similar and two ways in which they are different.

   a rectangle and parallelogram

   b parallelogram and rhombus

Unit 10, Week 1, Lesson 1

Multiplication HTO × O using the formal written method (1)

Use the formal written method to calculate HTO × O

Challenge 1

Write the multiples of 100 that each of these numbers comes between. Circle the multiple of 100 it is closest to.

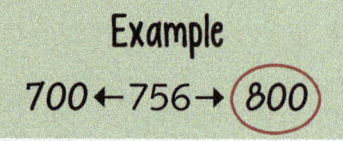

Example
700 ← 756 → (800)

851, 633, 163, 752, 271, 917, 543, 325, 229, 426

Challenge 2

Choose eight numbers from Challenge 1. Multiply four numbers by 2 and four numbers by 3. Estimate the answer first then use the formal written method to work out the answer.

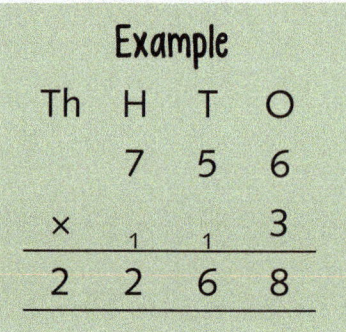

Example

Th	H	T	O
	7	5	6
×			3
	₁	₁	
2	2	6	8

Challenge 3

Multiply the two numbers alongside each other in the bottom row together to find the number above in the second row. Multiply the two numbers in the second row together to find the number at the top. Calculate the answers mentally for as long as you are able, then use the formal written method.

Example

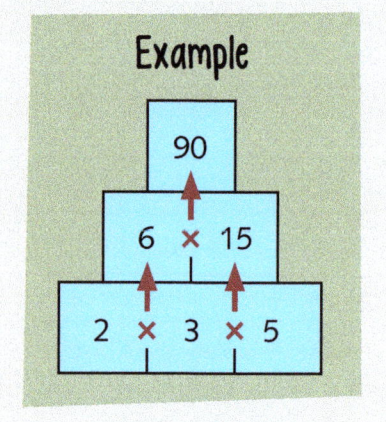

```
      90
      ↑
    6 × 15
    ↑   ↑
  2 × 3 × 5
```

a) 36, 4, 2

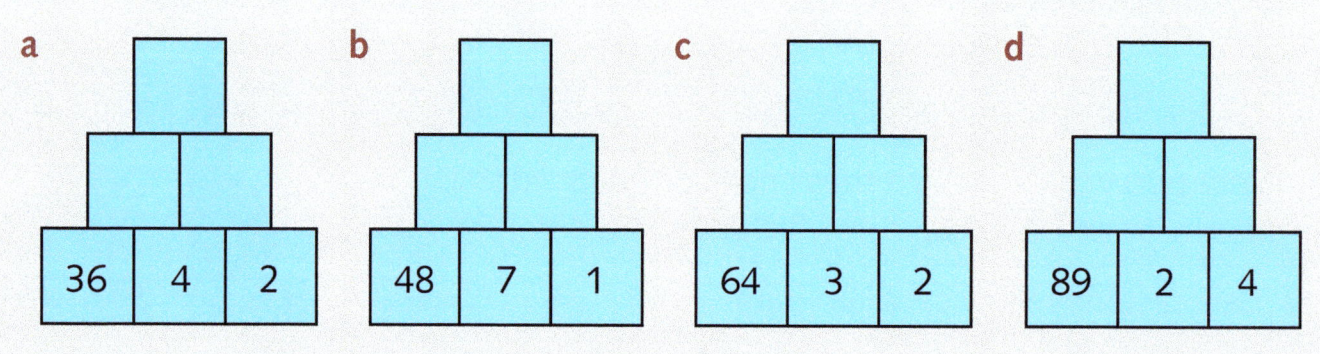

b) 48, 7, 1

c) 64, 3, 2

d) 89, 2, 4

Unit 10, Week 1, Lesson 2

Multiplication HTO × O using the formal written method (2)

Use the formal written method to calculate HTO × O

Challenge 1

1. Count back in multiples of the number in the box. Copy and complete each sequence.

   a 30   270, , , , , ,
   b 60   600, , , , , ,
   c 90   810, , , , , ,
   d 40   440, , , , , ,

2. Choose a multiple of 100 from box A and a multiple of 100 from box B. Add them together and write the answer. Make eight calculations. Choose different numbers each time.

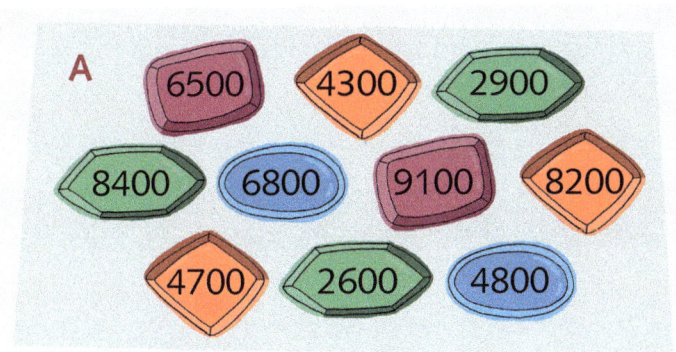

   A: 6500, 4300, 2900, 8400, 6800, 9100, 8200, 4700, 2600, 4800

   B: 600, 400, 800, 900, 500, 700, 300, 200

Challenge 2

1. Estimate the answer to each calculation.

   a 246 × 3   b 849 × 4   c 687 × 9   d 684 × 6
   e 263 × 8   f 473 × 7   g 549 × 5   h 736 × 8

2. Find the answer to each of the calculations above using the formal written method of multiplication. Check your answer is close to your estimated answer.

Example

$473 \times 7 \rightarrow 500 \times 7 = 3500$

Th	H	T	O
	4	7	3
×			7
3	3	1	1
	5	2	

Challenge 3

Find the missing numbers in these calculations.

a 463 × △ = 2315   b 257 × △ = 1028   c 337 × △ = 2022
d 835 × △ = 2505   e 476 × △ = 2380   f 736 × △ = 1472

Unit 10, Week 1, Lesson 3

Multiplication HTO × O using the most efficient method

Use the most efficient method to calculate HTO × O

Challenge 1

1. a 8 × 2
   b 80 × 2
   c 800 × 2

2. a 4 × 7
   b 40 × 7
   c 400 × 7

3. a 7 × 6
   b 70 × 6
   c 700 × 6

4. a 9 × 8
   b 90 × 8
   c 900 × 8

5. a 9 × 7
   b 90 × 7
   c 900 × 7

6. a 5 × 6
   b 50 × 6
   c 500 × 6

Challenge 2

Sort these calculations into two groups: those you would work out mentally and those where you would use a written method. Then work out the answer to each calculation using the most efficient method.

| 233 × 3 | 432 × 3 | 655 × 4 | 632 × 3 | 746 × 8 | 869 × 7 |
| 637 × 8 | 434 × 2 | 513 × 3 | 754 × 2 | 779 × 9 | 856 × 7 |

Challenge 3

Play this game with a partner. Each player chooses a number from the circles on the right.

Take turns to:
- roll the dice
- multiply the number on the dice by your chosen number
- choose the most appropriate method to calculate the answer, mental or written.

If you choose a written method, write the estimated answer first and then show your working out. Compare your answers each time. The player with the largest answer scores one point. The first player to score five points is the winner.

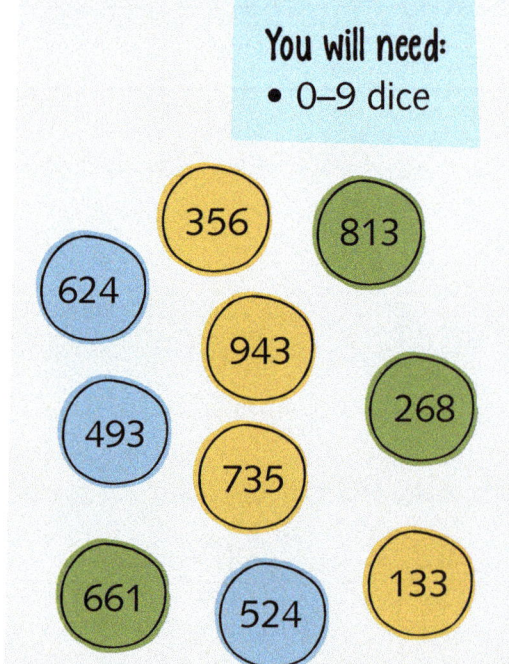

You will need:
- 0–9 dice

356, 813, 624, 943, 493, 268, 735, 661, 524, 133

Unit 10, Week 1, Lesson 4

Solving word problems (3)

Solve problems and reason mathematically

Challenge 1

Write the multiplication facts for each number coming out of the machine.

1. 4
    8
    7
    9
    × 6

2. 6
    9
    7
    8
    × 9

3. 9
    8
    6
    7
    × 7

Challenge 2

Use the information in the pictures to answer the questions.

a. The school buys 6 clarinets. What is the total cost?

b. The music teacher buys 6 guitars. How much do they cost altogether?

c. The school buys 3 keyboards and 3 drum kits. How much do they spend?

d. How much more does a drum kit cost than a keyboard?

e. If the school bought 1 of each of the string instruments what is the total cost?

f. The music club want to buy 1 of each item. How much money will they need?

g. How much change from €1000 do you get if you buy 5 violins?

Violin €168
Drum kit €852
Cello €537
Keyboard €439
Guitar €289
Clarinet €415

Challenge 3

Write your own word problems for these calculations. Swap them with a friend to solve.

a. 439 × 4
b. 1000 − 289
c. 852 + 289 + 168
d. 852 × 6

Unit 10, Week 2, Lesson 1

Equivalent fractions (3)

Use factors and multiples to recognise equivalent fractions and simplify fractions

Challenge 1

1 Continue the equivalent fraction pattern.

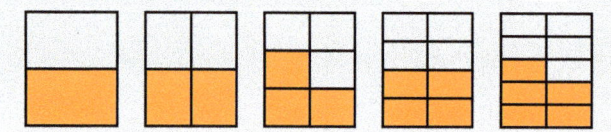

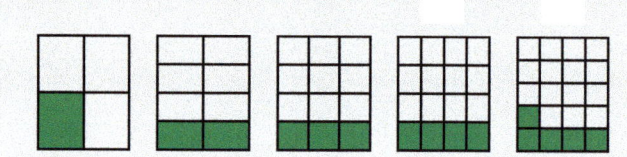

a $\frac{1}{2} = \frac{}{4} = \frac{}{6} = \frac{}{\square} = \frac{}{\square}$

b $\frac{1}{4} = \frac{}{8} = \frac{}{12} = \frac{}{\square} = \frac{}{\square}$

2 Explain what an equivalent fraction is.

Challenge 2

1 Continue the equivalent fraction pattern.

a $\frac{1}{5} = \frac{}{10} = \frac{}{\square} = \frac{}{\square} = \frac{}{\square} = \frac{}{\square}$

b $\frac{1}{6} = \frac{}{12} = \frac{}{\square} = \frac{}{\square} = \frac{}{\square} = \frac{}{\square}$

c $\frac{1}{7} = \frac{}{14} = \frac{}{\square} = \frac{}{\square} = \frac{}{\square} = \frac{}{\square}$

d $\frac{1}{8} = \frac{}{16} = \frac{}{\square} = \frac{}{\square} = \frac{}{\square} = \frac{}{\square}$

2 Simplify these fractions.

a $\frac{9}{18}$ b $\frac{6}{24}$ c $\frac{7}{28}$ d $\frac{8}{40}$ e $\frac{9}{54}$ f $\frac{6}{18}$

g $\frac{8}{56}$ h $\frac{6}{60}$ i $\frac{4}{48}$ j $\frac{9}{45}$ k $\frac{7}{77}$ l $\frac{20}{70}$

Challenge 3

1 Continue the equivalent fraction pattern for these non-unit fractions.

a $\frac{2}{3} = \frac{}{6} = \frac{}{9} = \frac{}{12} = \frac{}{15} = \frac{}{18}$

b $\frac{3}{5} = \frac{6}{\square} = \frac{}{\square} = \frac{}{\square} = \frac{}{\square} = \frac{}{\square}$

2 Simplify these fractions.

a $\frac{12}{60}$ b $\frac{10}{18}$ c $\frac{15}{25}$ d $\frac{36}{42}$ e $\frac{20}{50}$

f $\frac{32}{36}$ g $\frac{54}{90}$ h $\frac{44}{99}$ i $\frac{12}{21}$ j $\frac{14}{35}$

3 Explain why $\frac{12}{25}$ cannot be simplified?

20

Unit 10, Week 2, Lesson 2

Adding fractions

Add fractions with the same denominator

Challenge 1

Add these fractions. Use the pizzas to help you.

a $\frac{2}{4} + \frac{1}{4}$

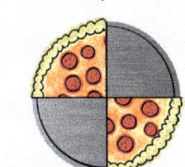

b $\frac{3}{5} + \frac{1}{5}$

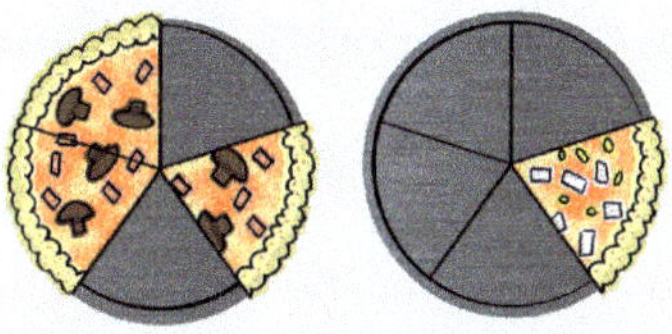

c $\frac{2}{6} + \frac{3}{6}$

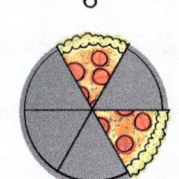

d $\frac{3}{8} + \frac{4}{8}$

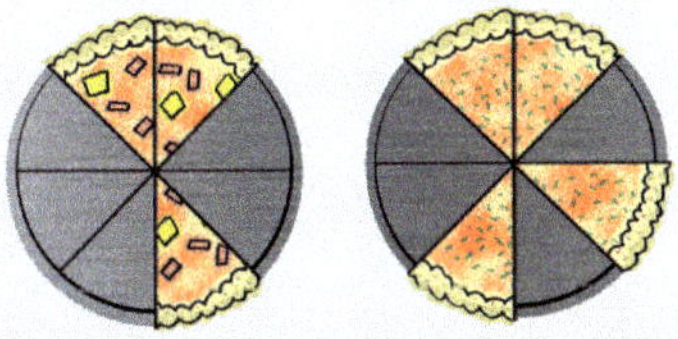

e $\frac{5}{7} + \frac{1}{7}$

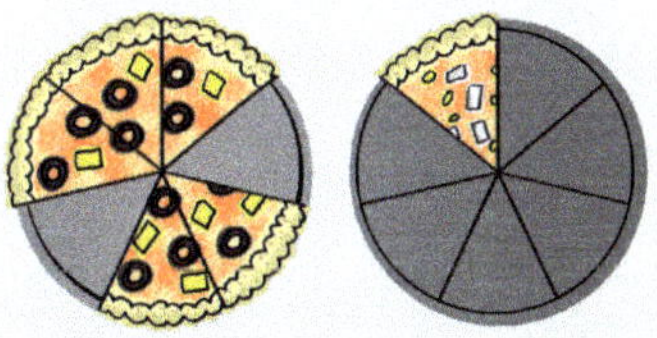

f $\frac{3}{10} + \frac{5}{10}$

Challenge 2

Add these fractions.

a $\frac{3}{7} + \frac{1}{7}$
b $\frac{5}{8} + \frac{2}{8}$
c $\frac{3}{9} + \frac{4}{9}$
d $\frac{2}{10} + \frac{7}{10}$
e $\frac{5}{7} + \frac{2}{7}$

f $\frac{3}{12} + \frac{6}{12}$
g $\frac{6}{10} + \frac{7}{10}$
h $\frac{8}{9} + \frac{4}{9}$
i $\frac{3}{3} + \frac{2}{3}$
j $\frac{8}{12} + \frac{5}{12}$

Challenge 3

1 Add these fractions.

a $\frac{11}{14} + \frac{2}{14}$
b $\frac{8}{13} + \frac{5}{13}$
c $\frac{9}{15} + \frac{7}{15}$
d $\frac{12}{100} + \frac{25}{100}$
e $\frac{13}{16} + \frac{5}{16}$

f $\frac{9}{14} + \frac{7}{14}$
g $\frac{5}{17} + \frac{15}{17}$
h $\frac{16}{100} + \frac{30}{100}$
i $\frac{15}{20} + \frac{8}{20}$
j $\frac{10}{18} + \frac{10}{18}$

2 Write these improper fractions as mixed numbers.

a $\frac{8}{6}$
b $\frac{12}{7}$
c $\frac{13}{9}$
d $\frac{8}{5}$
e $\frac{16}{10}$

f $\frac{14}{12}$
g $\frac{5}{4}$
h $\frac{11}{8}$
i $\frac{17}{11}$
j $\frac{16}{9}$

Example

$\frac{11}{8} = \frac{8}{8} + \frac{3}{8} = 1\frac{3}{8}$

Unit 10, Week 2, Lesson 3

Subtracting fractions

Subtract fractions with the same denominator

Challenge 1

Subtract these fractions.

a $\frac{4}{6} - \frac{1}{6}$ b $\frac{6}{7} - \frac{2}{7}$ c $\frac{8}{8} - \frac{5}{8}$ d $\frac{4}{5} - \frac{3}{5}$ e $\frac{7}{9} - \frac{5}{9}$

f $\frac{8}{10} - \frac{6}{10}$ g $\frac{3}{4} - \frac{1}{4}$ h $\frac{6}{8} - \frac{3}{8}$ i $\frac{8}{10} - \frac{7}{10}$ j $\frac{9}{12} - \frac{5}{12}$

Challenge 2

Subtract these fractions.

a $\frac{8}{9} - \frac{3}{9}$ b $\frac{11}{13} - \frac{8}{13}$ c $\frac{9}{10} - \frac{5}{10}$ d $\frac{7}{7} - \frac{5}{7}$ e $\frac{10}{12} - \frac{3}{12}$

f $\frac{9}{6} - \frac{4}{6}$ g $\frac{7}{5} - \frac{3}{5}$ h $\frac{10}{8} - \frac{6}{8}$ i $\frac{16}{15} - \frac{4}{15}$ j $\frac{11}{9} - \frac{10}{9}$

Challenge 3

1 Subtract these fractions.

a $\frac{11}{6} - \frac{4}{6}$ b $\frac{9}{8} - \frac{5}{8}$

c $\frac{15}{13} - \frac{7}{13}$ d $\frac{12}{10} - \frac{8}{10}$

e $\frac{14}{14} - \frac{12}{14}$ f $\frac{18}{10} - \frac{8}{10}$

g $\frac{113}{100} - \frac{20}{100}$ h $\frac{22}{20} - \frac{18}{20}$

2 Write these improper fractions as mixed numbers.

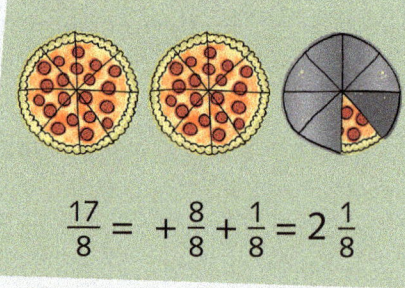

a $\frac{14}{6}$ b $\frac{13}{5}$ c $\frac{15}{14}$

d $\frac{11}{4}$ e $\frac{26}{10}$ f $\frac{7}{3}$

g $\frac{19}{8}$ h $\frac{9}{4}$ i $\frac{16}{7}$

Example

$\frac{17}{8} = + \frac{8}{8} + \frac{1}{8} = 2\frac{1}{8}$

Unit 10, Week 2, Lesson 4

Table fractions

Solve simple measure and money problems involving fractions

Challenge 1

What fraction of each chocolate bar will each child get if there are:

1. a 2 children at table A?
   b 6 children at table B?
2. a 3 children at table A?
   b 5 children at table B?
3. a 4 children at table A?
   b 4 children at table B?

Challenge 2

What fraction of each chocolate bar will each child get if there are:

1. a 2 children at table A?
   b 4 children at table B?
   c 4 children at table C?
2. a 3 children at table A?   b 2 children at table B?   c 5 children at table C?
3. a 1 child at table A?   b 3 children at table B?   c 6 children at table C?

Challenge 3

What fraction of each chocolate bar will each child get if there are:

1. a 4 children at table A?
   b 2 children at table B?
   c 6 children at table C?
2. a 5 children at table A?
   b 4 children at table B?
   c 3 children at table C?

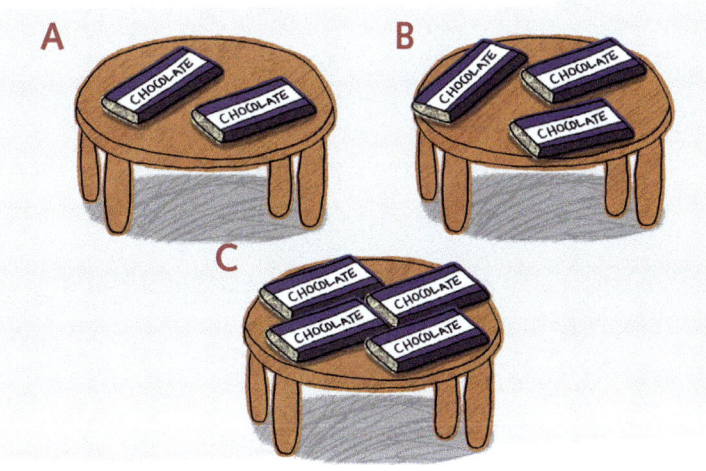

Unit 10, Week 3, Lesson 1

Filling station litres

Use the relationships between litres and millilitres to record capacity using decimals

Example
7600 ml = 7000 ml + 600 ml
= 7 l 600 ml
= 7·6 l
= 7 $\frac{6}{10}$ l

Challenge 1

Write the capacity of each container in four different ways.

a 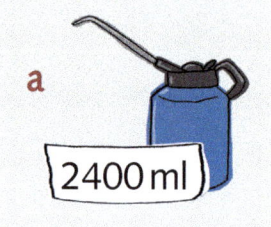 2400 ml
b  4500 ml
c  5300 ml
d 9800 ml

Challenge 2

1 Write these amounts in litres.

a 3500 ml   b 2700 ml   c 4200 ml
d 1900 ml   e 5600 ml   f 6800 ml

Example
4300 ml = 4000 ml + 300 ml
= 4·3 l

2 Write these amounts in litres.

a 6250 ml   b 9750 ml   c 6510 ml
d 8980 ml   e 7020 ml   f 10050 ml

3 Write these capacities in millilitres.

a 7·47 l   b 5·82 l   c 6·09 l
d 5·13 l   e 9·95 l   f 10·66 l

Challenge 3

The car mechanic has three metal jugs. The first jug will hold 3 litres. The second jug will hold 5 litres. The third jug is much larger than the other two jugs. Explain how the mechanic can use the three jugs to measure exactly 4 litres of brake fluid.

3 l   5 l

24

Unit 10, Week 3, Lesson 2

Science lab litres

Use multiplication to convert from larger to smaller units

Example
3·75 l = 3000 ml + 750 ml
     = 3750 ml

Challenge 1

Write the capacity of each flask in millilitres.

a 4·25 l
b 5·34 l
c 2·73 l
d 3·69 l
e 3·08 l

Challenge 2

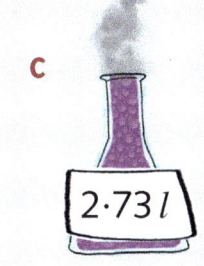

Professor Mack has five measuring jugs and an empty container.

He has mislaid his other measuring jugs but he can use these jugs more than once.

Jugs: 50 ml, 250 ml, 100 ml, 750 ml, 500 ml

Explain how he can pour 1 litre of water into an empty container using:

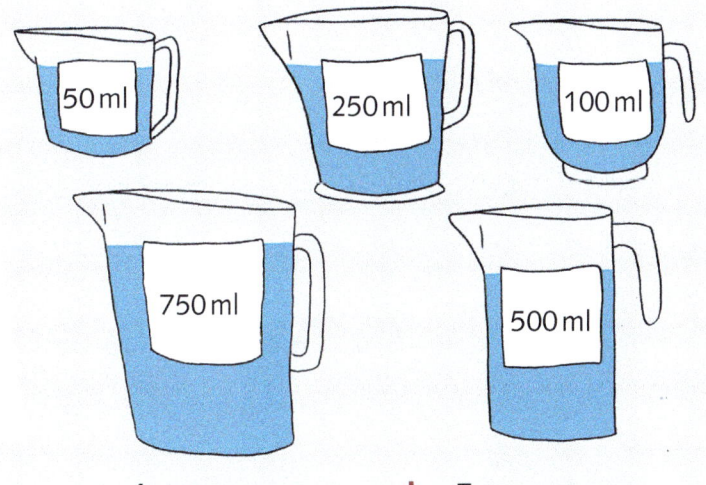

a 2 measures   b 3 measures   c 4 measures   d 5 measures

Challenge 3

The table shows the amount of water, tea and milk a science student had each day.

Use the information in the pictures to work out how many millilitres of liquid he drank each day.

Day	Bottles of water	Mugs of tea	Small cartons of milk
Monday	3	2	1
Tuesday	2	3	2
Wednesday	1	4	3
Thursday	3	3	4
Friday	2	1	5

Mug: 0·2 l
Bottle: 0·5 l
Milk carton: 0·1 l

Unit 10, Week 3, Lesson 3

Estimating and rounding capacity

Estimate and compare capacity and round numbers on measuring jugs

Challenges 1, 2

1 Estimate the amount of liquid in each bottle to the nearest 100 ml.

   a, b, 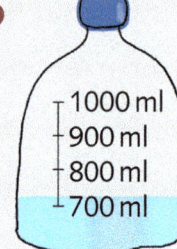 c, 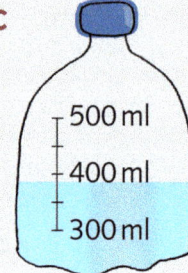 d

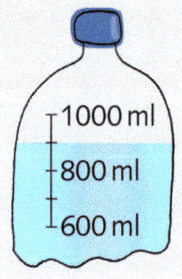

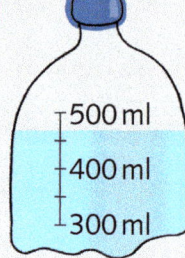

2 Round the amount of liquid in each container to the nearest litre.

   a 4·2 l   b 5·3 l   c 2·8 l   d 6·6 l

Challenge 2

For each of the four measuring jugs write the amount of liquid:

   a in millilitres
   b rounded to the nearest 100 ml

   A, B, 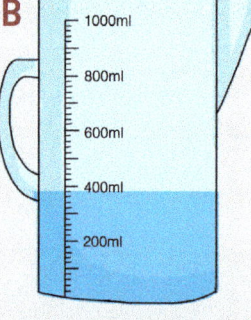 C, 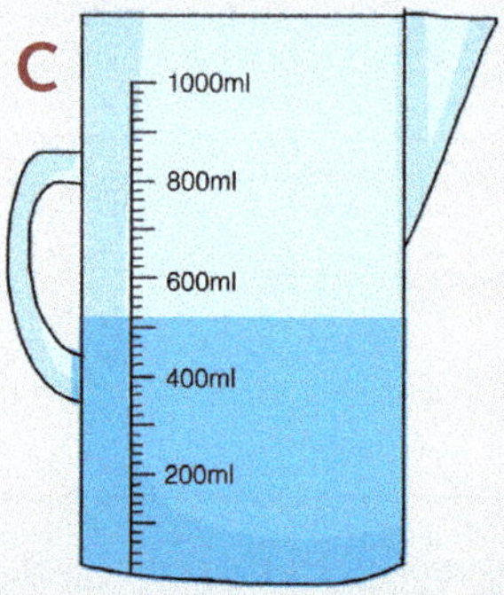 D

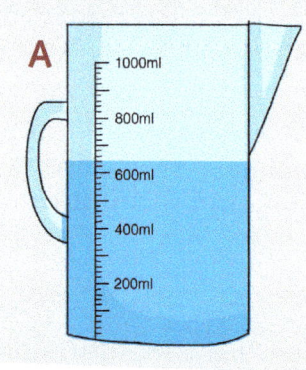

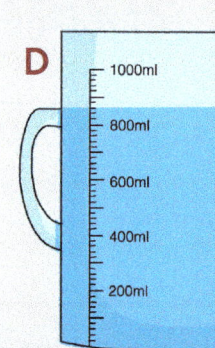

Challenge 3

The table shows the engine capacity of a family car. Copy and complete the table for cars with these engine capacities.

   a 1612 ml   b 1775 ml
   c 1990 ml   d 2235 ml

Capacity in ml	Rounded to nearest: 10 ml	Rounded to nearest: 100 ml	Capacity in litres
1385	1390	1400	1·4

Unit 10, Week 3, Lesson 4

Litres of juice

Calculate different measures of capacity using decimals to 2 places

Challenge 1

Find the number of times you can fill the measuring jug from the bottle beside it.

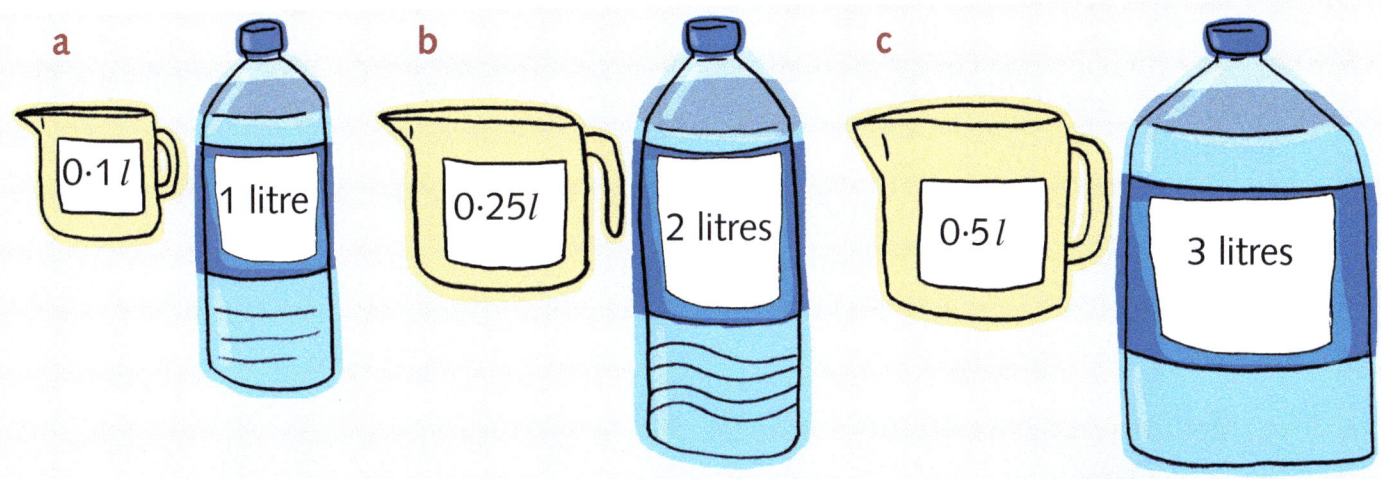

a 0·1 *l* jug / 1 litre bottle
b 0·25 *l* jug / 2 litres bottle
c 0·5 *l* jug / 3 litres bottle

Challenges 2, 3

Look at the instructions on the bottle of blackcurrant juice. Copy and complete the table.

Mix 1 measure of juice with 4 measures of water.

Blackcurrant juice	Water	Amount of drink made
0·1 *l*	0·4 *l*	0·5 *l*
0·15 *l*		
0·25 *l*		
0·33 *l*		
	2 *l*	
0·67 *l*		
	3 *l*	
1·5 *l*		

Challenge 3

The blackcurrant juice is also sold in 0·33 *l* cartons. How many litres are there in:

a 1 pack of 6 cartons?

b 10 packs of 6 cartons?

Unit 11, Week 1, Lesson 1

Meet the target (1)

- Add numbers with up to 4 digits using the formal written method of columnar addition
- Estimate and use inverse operations to check answers to a calculation

You will need:
- 0–9 dice

Challenge 1

1. Your target is to get an answer as close to 1000 as possible.

   Roll the dice six times and decide where to write each digit. Then work out the answer to the calculation. Do this ten times.

2. Which of your calculations is closest to 1000?

Rule

Record your calculations like this:

H T O
☐ ☐ ☐
+ ☐ ☐ ☐

Challenge 2

1. Your target is to get an answer as close to 8000 as possible.

   Roll the dice eight times and decide where to write each digit. Then work out the answer to the calculation. Do this ten times.

2. Which of your calculations is closest to 8000? Explain how you know.

Rule

Record your calculations like this:

Th H T O
☐ ☐ ☐ ☐
+ ☐ ☐ ☐ ☐

Challenge 3

1. Your target is to get an answer as close to 12 000 as possible.

   Roll the dice eight times and decide where to write each digit. Then work out the answer to the calculation. Do this ten times.

2. Which of your calculations is closest to 12 000? Explain how you know.

Rule

Record your calculations like this:

Th H T O
☐ ☐ ☐ ☐
+ ☐ ☐ ☐ ☐

Unit 11, Week 1, Lesson 2

Meet the target (2)

- Subtract numbers with up to 4 digits using the formal written method of columnar subtraction
- Estimate and use inverse operations to check answers to a calculation

You will need:
- 0–9 dice

Challenge 1

1. Your target is to get an answer as close to 400 as possible.

   Roll the dice six times and decide where to write each digit. Then work out the answer to the calculation. Do this ten times.

2. Which of your calculations is closest to 400?

Rule

Record your calculations like this:

H T O
☐ ☐ ☐
− ☐ ☐ ☐

Challenge 2

1. Your target is to get an answer as close to 4000 as possible.

   Roll the dice eight times and decide where to write each digit. Then work out the answer to the calculation. Do this ten times.

2. Which of your calculations is closest to 4000? Explain how you know.

Rule

Record your calculations like this:

Th H T O
☐ ☐ ☐ ☐
− ☐ ☐ ☐ ☐

Challenge 3

1. Your target is to get an answer as close to 5000 as possible.

   Roll the dice eight times and decide where to write each digit. Then work out the answer to the calculation. Do this ten times.

2. Which of your calculations is closest to 5000? Explain how you know.

Rule

Record your calculations like this:

Th H T O
☐ ☐ ☐ ☐
− ☐ ☐ ☐ ☐

Unit 11, Week 1, Lesson 3

Ordering and subtracting money

Order and calculate with money in euros and cents

Challenge 1

1. Copy out these amounts and write an amount in the spaces, still keeping the order.

   a €4.67,　　　, €4.89,　　　, €5.00,　　　, €5.15

   b €15.25,　　　, €15.50,　　　, €15.55,　　　, €15.75

   c €20.47,　　　, €20.63,　　　, €20.80,　　　, €20.90

2. Subtract these amounts of money mentally.

   a €10.00 – €5.30　　　b €14.00 – €3.40　　　c €17.00 – €8.60

3. Subtract these amounts using the formal written method.

   a €28.48 – €12.36　　　b €36.74 – €15.38　　　c €34.38 – €27.15

Challenge 2

1. Copy out these amounts and write an amount in the spaces, still keeping the order.

   a €51.15,　　　, €51.51,　　　, €51.80,　　　, €51.99,　　　, €52.10

   b €63.03,　　　, €63.06,　　　, €63.36,　　　, €63.52,　　　, €63.68

2. Subtract these amounts of money mentally.

   a €50.00 – €24.50　　　b €65.00 – €31.20　　　c €68.40 – €42.00

3. Subtract these amounts of money using the formal written method.

   a €94.38 – €67.18　　　b €135.44 – €128.22　　　c €153.85 – €127.49

Challenge 3

1. Using the digits on the cards make ten different amounts of money. Remember, they all need to be €HTO.th, such as €489.23.

2. Write your amounts in order, smallest to largest.

3. Using your amounts, write ten subtraction calculations.

Unit 11, Week 1, Lesson 4

Lunch problems

Solve problems in contexts, deciding which operations and methods to use and why

Use these clues to find out what Chris, Joe and Marsha chose for lunch today.

- They all had different fillings and different types of bread.
- The sandwich fillings were cheese, tuna or beef.
- The bread was brown, white or a granary roll.
- Chris only eats beef if he has white bread.
- Joe never eats beef.
- Marsha had a roll yesterday so she chose something different.
- Joe had an egg sandwich yesterday.
- Chris likes tuna but didn't want it for lunch.
- Joe had white bread.

Work with a partner. Talk to your partner about each of the clues. How will you organise your working out?

Which bread and filling did each of the three children choose for lunch?

When you know what each of the three children chose, use these clues to work out how much they paid and how much change they each got.

- One child has €2, one has €5 and one has €10.
- Joe has the most money.
- The prices are €2.65, €1.95 and €2.43.
- Chris's lunch was the cheapest.
- Marsha's lunch cost just over half of her money.
- Chris only just had enough money.

Choose two or three characters of your own. Decide what they buy when they go into the café. Write some clues for a partner to use to solve your problem.

Unit 11, Week 2, Lesson 1

Decimal tenths and hundredths

- Recognise and write decimal equivalents of any number of tenths and hundredths
- Recognise and write decimal equivalents to $\frac{1}{4}, \frac{1}{2}, \frac{3}{4}$

Challenge 1

1 Write the decimal tenth equivalent to these fractions.

(number line from 0 to 1 with marks at $\frac{1}{10}, \frac{2}{10}, \frac{3}{10}, \frac{4}{10}, \frac{5}{10}, \frac{6}{10}, \frac{7}{10}, \frac{8}{10}, \frac{9}{10}$; labelled below 0, 0·1, a, b, c, d, e, f, g, h, 1)

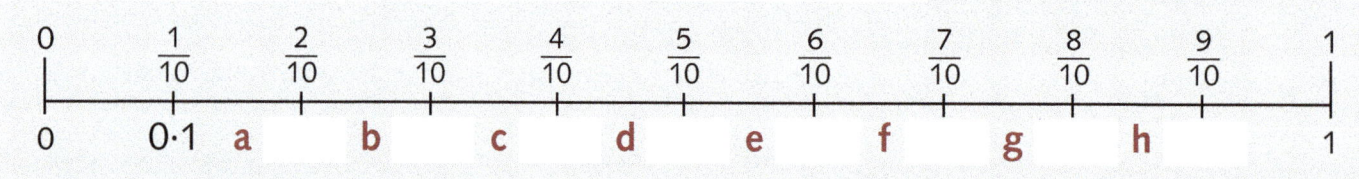

2 Count the hundredths that are shaded blue and record them as a fraction and a decimal fraction.

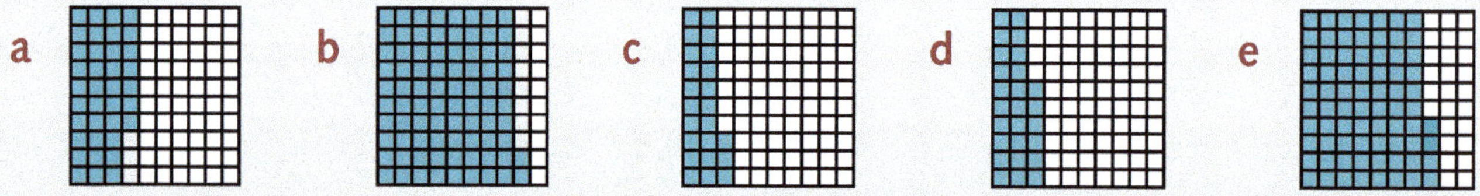

a   b   c   d   e

Challenge 2

1 Write the decimal fraction that is equivalent to these fractions.

a $\frac{7}{10}$ b $\frac{5}{10}$ c $\frac{3}{10}$ d $\frac{9}{10}$

e $\frac{71}{100}$ f $\frac{12}{100}$ g $\frac{63}{100}$ h $\frac{58}{100}$

2 Write the fraction that is equivalent to these decimal fractions.

a 0·4   b 0·1   c 0·8   d 0·2

e 0·3   f 0·28   g 0·17   h 0·55

3 Draw a 12 cm number line. Draw intervals at 0 cm, 3 cm, 6 cm, 9 cm and 12 cm. Mark the 0 cm interval '0' and the 12 cm interval '1'. Use the number line to record these fractions and decimals in the correct places.

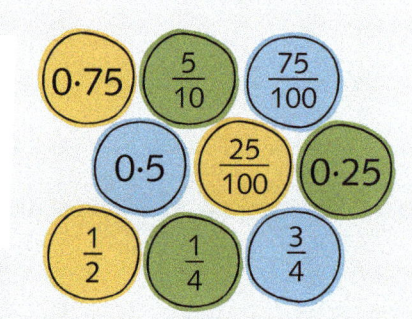

0·75 $\frac{5}{10}$ $\frac{75}{100}$ 0·5 $\frac{25}{100}$ 0·25 $\frac{1}{2}$ $\frac{1}{4}$ $\frac{3}{4}$

Challenge 3

Write the decimal values for the arrows marked on the number line.

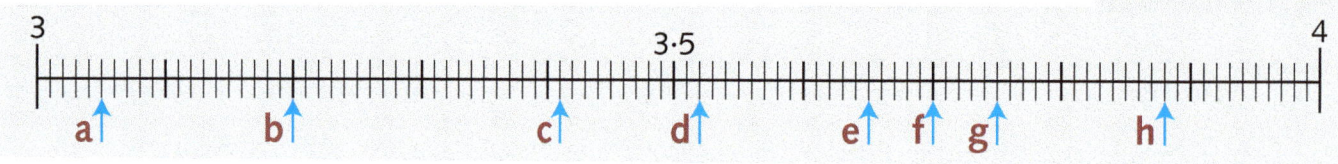

(number line from 3 to 4 with 3·5 marked; arrows a, b, c, d, e, f, g, h)

Unit 11, Week 2, Lesson 2

Comparing and rounding decimals

- Compare decimals with up to 2 places
- Round decimals with 1 decimal place to the nearest whole number

Challenge 1

1 Count on ten hundredths from each of these decimals.

   a 4·2   b 3·65   c 4·18   d 7·1   e 5·53
   f 7·26   g 8·5   h 9·41   i 11·3   j 12·5

2 Round these decimals to the nearest whole number.

   a 2·7   b 3·9   c 7·5   d 8·3   e 9·6
   f 10·4   g 12·5   h 12·1   i 14·8   j 15·2

Challenge 2

1 Order these decimal numbers, smallest to largest.

   a 4·5, 4·9, 4·1, 4·7, 4·4   b 6·87, 6·08, 6·88, 6·18, 6·48
   c 8·46, 7·48, 8·14, 7·53, 7·21, 8·05   d 12·64, 12·81, 12·46, 12·66, 12·18
   e 16·61, 16·16, 16·66, 16·11, 16·01   f 18·4, 19·1, 18·7, 19·5, 18·3

2 Write the two whole numbers each of these decimals comes between.
   Then circle the whole number that the decimal number rounds up or down to.

   a 13·4   b 18·2   c 16·9   d 11·1
   e 15·7   f 19·5   g 25·6   h 28·8

Challenge 3

1 Fill in the spaces with decimal numbers, keeping the numbers in order.

   a 13·8,   , 14·1,   ,   , 14·8,   ,   , 15·3
   b 15·99,   , 16·06,   ,   , 16·36,   , 16·51
   c 20·01,   ,   , 20·09,   ,   , 20·19,   , 20·29
   d 23·7,   , 23·9,   ,   , 24·9,   ,   , 25·1

2 Explain the rule for rounding numbers with 1 decimal place.

3 Jasmine is 1·4 metres tall, rounded to 1 decimal place
   and Jim is 1·39 metres tall. Jasmine is actually smaller than Jim.
   Explain how this can be.

Unit 11, Week 2, Lesson 3

Dividing by 10 and 100

Divide 1 and 2-digit numbers by 10 and 100

Challenge 1

Divide these numbers by 10.

a 5   b 9   c 8   d 2
e 28 f 51 g 83 h 35
i 47 j 64 k 91 l 76

Hints

Tens	Ones	.	tenths
	6		
	0	.	6

Tens	Ones	.	tenths
2	9		
	2	.	9

Challenge 2

Divide these numbers by 100.

a 5   b 63 c 91
d 78 e 3   f 42
g 75 h 1   i 44
j 57 k 36 l 89

Hints

Tens	Ones	.	tenths	hundredths
	8			
	0	.	0	8

Tens	Ones	.	tenths	hundredths
3	7			
	0	.	3	7

Challenge 3

1 Work out these calculations.

a 48 ÷ 10   b 95 ÷ 100   c 3 ÷ 10
d 64 ÷ 100   e 20 ÷ 10   f 173 ÷ 10
g 284 ÷ 100 h 301 ÷ 10   i 484 ÷ 10

2 Explain what happens to the digits in a number when you divide the number by 10.

3 What happens when you divide a number by 100?

Unit 11, Week 2, Lesson 4

Decimal problems

Solve simple measure and money problems involving decimals to 2 places

Challenge 1

1. Using the information in the table to the right, put the runners in order, starting with the fastest.

2. Copy this number line. Write the times on the number line.

   26   27   28   29

3. Every runner wants to run 3 seconds faster next time. Write down their targets.

Name	Time (seconds)
Billy	26·3
Poppy	28·2
Rosie	26·9
Stanley	27·5
Julian	28·7

Challenge 2

1. Using the information in the table to the right, put all the children in order, heaviest to lightest.

2. All the children predict that in a year's time they will be 5 kg heavier. How much will they all weigh then?

3. Which two children's weights are the closest together? Put all the weights on a number line if this helps.

Name	Weight (kilograms)
Susie	38·25
Max	36·95
Olly	38·05
Jessie	34·67
Monty	36·54

Challenge 3

Look at the table to the right.

1. If every child rounded their money to the nearest euro, what would their amounts be?

2. Which two children's amounts of money are the closest together?

3. If every child saved another €7, how much would they have?

Name	Money saved (€)
Yasmin	47.83
Maisha	49.03
Hussain	48.28
Mark	47.24
Penny	48.96

Unit 11, Week 3, Lesson 1

Take off coordinates

Use coordinates to describe the position of a point on a grid in the first quadrant

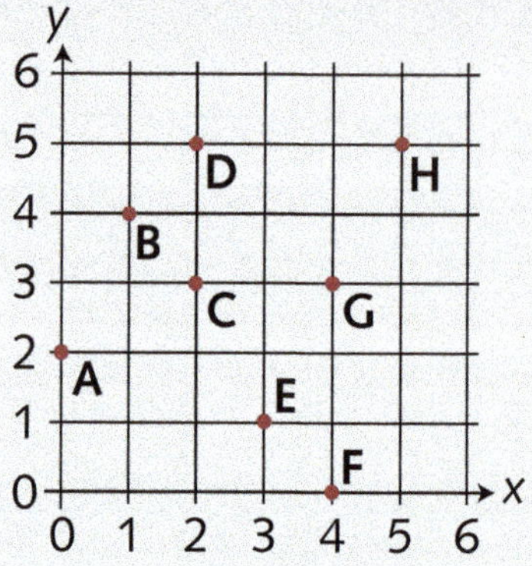

Challenge 1

1. The grid shows the position of some moon craters. Write the coordinates of craters **B**, **C** and **D**.

2. Copy and complete these sentences.

    a Craters with an x-coordinate of 4 are
      F (4,   ) and   (,   ).

    b Crater   has the same x-coordinate and y-coordinate.

Example
Crater **A** (0, 2)

Challenges 2, 3

1. The coordinates are joined to make a picture. Write the coordinates in order.

    (0, 3) → (1, 3) → (,) → (,)
    → (,) → (,) → (0, 3)

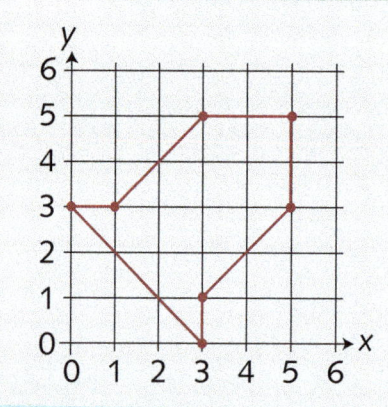

2. Use Resource 15: 9 × 9 coordinate grids. Draw a picture by joining these coordinates in order.

    (2, 8) → (8, 2) → (3, 2) → (2, 1) →
    (1, 1) → (1, 2) → (2, 3) → (2, 8)

You will need:
- Resource 15: 9 × 9 coordinate grids
- ruler

Challenge 3

1. This picture shows half of a symmetrical star.

    a Copy and complete the star

    b Write the coordinates for each new point

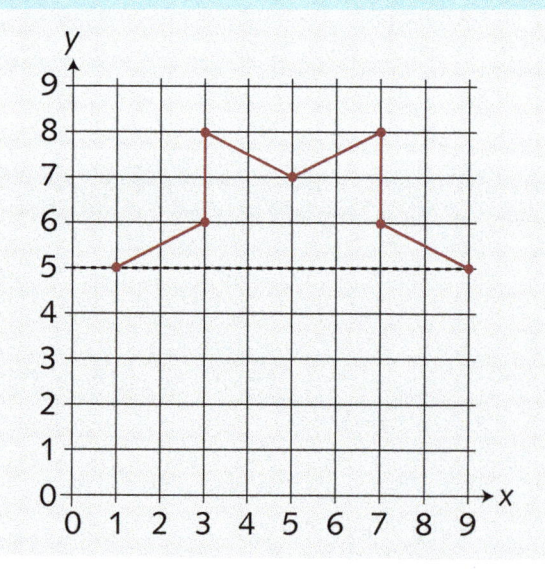

Unit 11, Week 3, Lesson 2

Constellation coordinates

Plot specified points and join them to make a 2-D shape

You will need:
- Resource 15: 9 × 9 coordinate grids
- red pencil
- ruler

Challenges 2, 3

Use Resource 15: 9 × 9 coordinate grids. Plot and label these points to find the six stars in Constellation Hex.

   A (5, 9)   B (9, 9)   C (9, 5)
   D (5, 0)   E (1, 1)   F (0, 5)

Challenge 2

1 a Draw straight lines joining the stars in order:
      A to B, B to C and so on back to A.

   b Name the 2-D shape you make.

2 a Draw two straight lines joining stars A to C and B to E.

   b A black hole lies at the intersection of these lines.
      Write its coordinates as: BH (,)

3 Use your red pencil to draw straight lines joining the stars:

   a A → C → E → A   b B → D → F → B

   c Name the shape enclosed by the red lines.

4 a Find the intersection of the lines joining stars A to D and F to C.

   b Move 3 squares left and 2 squares up. This is where a supernova lies.

   c Write the coordinates of the supernova as: S (,)

Challenge 3

1 A comet is travelling in a straight line from star D to star F. What might its coordinates be?

2 Investigate what happens to Constellation Hex when you double both coordinates of each star.

Unit 11, Week 3, Lesson 3

Coordinates of shapes

Use coordinates to describe the position of a point on a grid in the first quadrant

Challenge 1

Write the coordinates of:

a   parallelogram **PQRS**

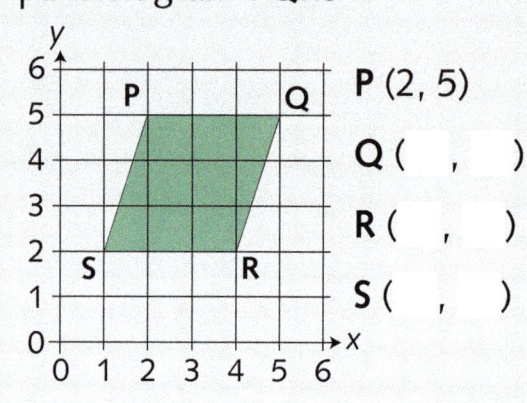

P (2, 5)
Q (,)
R (,)
S (,)

b   trapezium **TUVW**

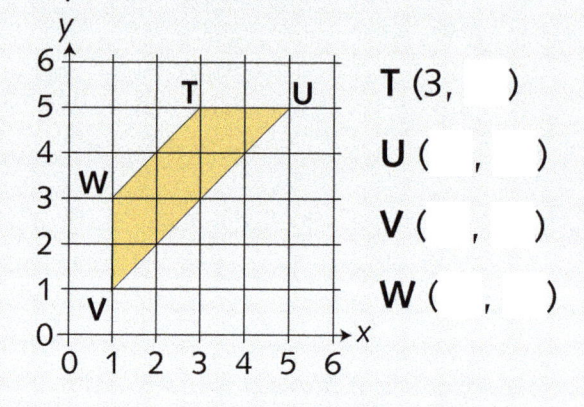

T (3,)
U (,)
V (,)
W (,)

Challenge 2

1   For each half shape below:

   a   copy it on to a 6 × 6 coordinate grid

   b   reflect the shape in the dotted red line of symmetry

You will need:
- Resource 14: 6 × 6 coordinate grids
- ruler
- red pencil

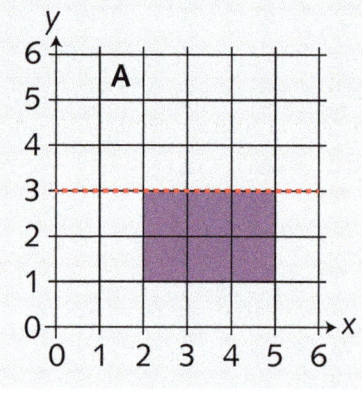

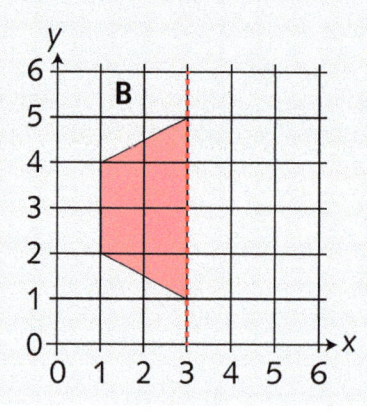

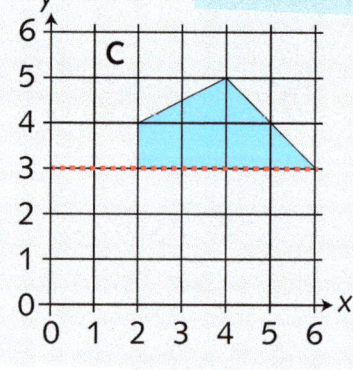

2   Name each whole shape and write its coordinates.

Challenge 3

Investigate what happens to shapes **PQRS** and **TUVW** from Challenge 1 when you:

   a   add three to both the *x*- and *y*-coordinates

   b   swap over the numbers for the *x*- and *y*-coordinates

You will need:
- 1 cm squared paper

or

- Coordinates tool

Unit 11, Week 3, Lesson 4

Plotting points and making shapes

Plot specified points and join them to make a 2-D shape

You will need:
- Resource 14: 6 × 6 coordinate grids
- ruler

or
- Coordinates tool

Challenge 1

a Plot these points on a 6 × 6 coordinate grid:

A (1, 2) **B** (5, 2) **C** (5, 6)

b **ABCD** is a square. Write the coordinates of **D**.

c Join the points in order to complete the square.

Challenges 2, 3

1 a Plot these two sets of points on a 6 × 6 coordinate grid:

Set A (1, 3) (1, 5) (3, 5)   **Set B** (3, 1) (5, 1) (5, 3)

b Join the three points in each set to make two right angles.

c Complete the shape by drawing two parallel lines.

d Name the shape you have made.

2 a Plot these points: **A** (1, 1) **B** (1, 3) **C** (3, 6) **D** (5, 3)

b Join the points **A** to **B**, **B** to **C** and **C** to **D**.

c The shape **ABCDE** is a pentagon with two right angles. Write the coordinates of the point **E**.

d Join **D** to **E** and **E** to **A**.

Challenge 3

1 Draw a picture in a 6 × 6 coordinate grid.

2 Investigate what happens to your picture when you:

a double the x-coordinate of the points

b double the y-coordinate of the points

c double both coordinate numbers

Unit 12, Week 1, Lesson 1

Division TO ÷ O using partitioning

Use partitioning to calculate TO ÷ O

Challenge 1

In each set of balloons, find the multiples of the number on the label.

a) Label: **60** — 60, 210, 480, 300, 120, 320, 70, 240, 540, 250

b) Label: **90** — 720, 630, 200, 410, 540, 440, 160, 270, 180, 360

c) Label: **80** — 240, 120, 640, 60, 560, 400, 320, 600, 80, 420

d) Label: **70** — 630, 100, 150, 180, 280, 350, 200, 490, 210, 420

Challenge 2

1 a	66 ÷ 6	b	660 ÷ 6	2 a	40 ÷ 8	b 400 ÷ 8
3 a	18 ÷ 2	b	180 ÷ 2	4 a	32 ÷ 4	b 320 ÷ 4
5 a	32 ÷ 8	b	320 ÷ 8	6 a	24 ÷ 6	b 240 ÷ 6
7 a	27 ÷ 3	b	270 ÷ 3	8 a	35 ÷ 7	b 350 ÷ 7
9 a	54 ÷ 9	b	540 ÷ 9	10 a	20 ÷ 2	b 200 ÷ 2

Challenge 3

Partition each of these numbers to help you find the answer to the division calculations.

a) 76 ÷ 4   b) 96 ÷ 6   c) 92 ÷ 4
d) 84 ÷ 6   e) 96 ÷ 2   f) 91 ÷ 7

Example
$$81 ÷ 3 = (60 + 21) ÷ 3$$
$$= 20 + 7$$
$$= 27$$

Unit 12, Week 1, Lesson 2

Division TO ÷ O using the formal written method

Use the formal written method to calculate TO ÷ O

Challenge 1

Write the division fact for each number coming out of the machine.

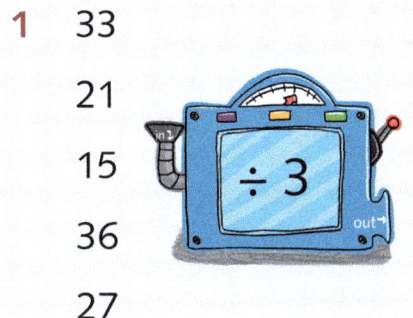

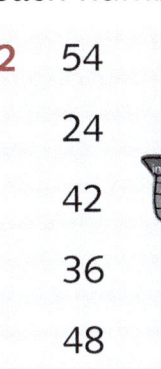

1. 33, 21, 15, 36, 27 ÷ 3

2. 54, 24, 42, 36, 48 ÷ 6

3. 72, 36, 63, 54, 81 ÷ 9

Challenges 2, 3

1. Approximate the answer to each calculation.

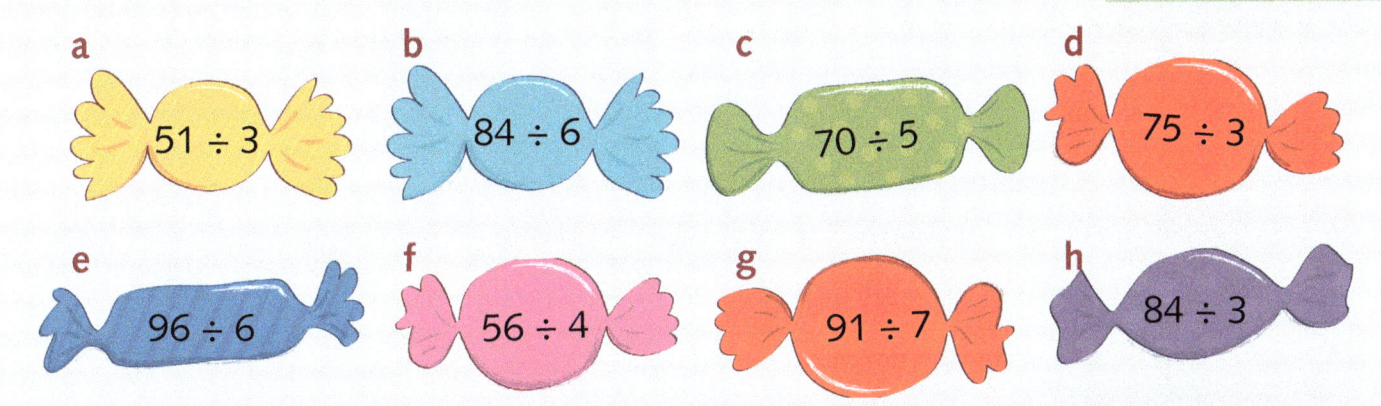

> **Example**
> 92 ÷ 4 → 25

a. 51 ÷ 3
b. 84 ÷ 6
c. 70 ÷ 5
d. 75 ÷ 3
e. 96 ÷ 6
f. 56 ÷ 4
g. 91 ÷ 7
h. 84 ÷ 3

2. Find the answer to each of the calculations in Question 1 using the formal written method.

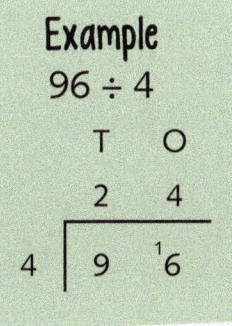

> **Example**
> 96 ÷ 4
>
> ```
>      T  O
>      2  4
>   4 | 9  ¹6
> ```

Challenge 3

Check your answers to each calculation in Challenges 2, 3 using the inverse operation. Choose the method of multiplication you find the easiest.

Unit 12, Week 1, Lesson 3

Division HTO ÷ O using partitioning

Use partitioning to calculate HTO ÷ O

Challenge 1

1. a 8 ÷ 2
   b 80 ÷ 2
   c 800 ÷ 2

2. a 42 ÷ 7
   b 420 ÷ 7
   c 4200 ÷ 7

3. a 48 ÷ 8
   b 480 ÷ 8
   c 4800 ÷ 8

4. a 54 ÷ 6
   b 540 ÷ 6
   c 5400 ÷ 6

Challenge 2

1. Choose three numbers from the circles. Divide each number by 3 using the mental partitioning method of division.

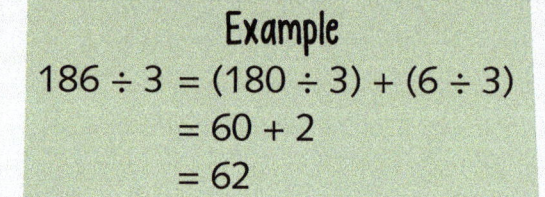

> **Example**
> 186 ÷ 3 = (180 ÷ 3) + (6 ÷ 3)
> = 60 + 2
> = 62

246   273   213   189   156   129

2. Choose three numbers from the circles. Divide each number by 6 using the mental partitioning method of division.

366   486   606   726   660   486

3. Choose three numbers from the circles. Divide each number by 4 using the mental partitioning method of division.

124   168   244   288   448   364

Challenge 3

1. Oh no! The ink pot has spilled. Find the missing numbers.

   a 164 ÷ 4 = ▆
   b 279 ÷ ▆ = 93
   c 455 ÷ 5 = ▆
   d 246 ÷ ▆ = 41
   e 369 ÷ ▆ = 41
   f 208 ÷ 4 = ▆
   g 364 ÷ 4 = ▆
   h ▆ ÷ 7 = 71
   i ▆ ÷ 8 = 31

2. Explain how you worked out the numbers covered by the ink in questions **h** and **i**.

Unit 12, Week 1, Lesson 4

Division using the expanded written method

Use the expanded written method to calculate HTO ÷ O

Challenge 1

1 Write the multiple of 6 that comes before each of these numbers.

   a 22   b 55   c 67   d 34   e 50

2 Write the multiple of 8 that comes before each of these numbers.

   a 20   b 75   c 51   d 65   e 9

3 Write the multiple of 7 that comes before each of these numbers.

   a 23   b 50   c 86   d 43   e 24

Challenges 2, 3

Work out the answer to each calculation using the expanded written method of division. Remember to estimate the answer first.

1 a 258 ÷ 3   b 192 ÷ 3
   c 144 ÷ 3   d 285 ÷ 3

2 a 375 ÷ 5   b 465 ÷ 5
   c 270 ÷ 5   d 185 ÷ 5

3 a 372 ÷ 6   b 198 ÷ 6
   c 264 ÷ 6   d 558 ÷ 6

4 a 198 ÷ 9   b 387 ÷ 9
   c 666 ÷ 9   d 495 ÷ 9

Example

252 ÷ 3 → 80

```
      H T O
        8 4
     ┌──────
   3 │ 2 5 2
       2 4 0   (80 × 3)
       ─────
         1 2
         1 2   (4 × 3)
       ─────
           0
```

Challenge 3

Check your answers from Challenges 2, 3 using the inverse operation. Choose the method of multiplication you find the easiest.

Unit 12, Week 2, Lesson 1

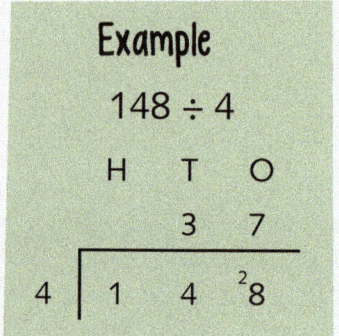

Division using the formal written method (1)

Use the formal written method to calculate HTO ÷ O

Challenge 1

1 These calculations are incomplete. Write the missing number.

   a 54 ÷ 9 = ☐   b 48 ÷ ☐ = 8   c ☐ ÷ 9 = 3
   d ☐ ÷ 4 = 6   e 21 ÷ 7 = ☐   f 36 ÷ ☐ = 6

2 These calculations are also incomplete. One or more digits are missing. Write the missing digits.

   a ☐4 ÷ 8 = 8   b ☐6 ÷ ☐ = 9   c 3☐ ÷ 4 = 8
   d 2☐ ÷ 4 = 7   e ☐6 ÷ ☐ = 11   f 7☐ ÷ ☐ = 10

3 Find the 10 times multiple of the number at the top of the column that is closest to, but less than, each of the 3-digit numbers.

4	6	7	9
148	138	168	216
116	204	245	171
132	174	273	288

Example
10 times multiple of 4 closest to, but less than, 148.
10 × 4 = 40
20 × 4 = 80
30 × 4 = 120 ⟶ 148

Challenges 2, 3

Choose two 3-digit numbers from each column in Question 3 of Challenge 1. Divide the 3-digit number by the 1-digit number in the box at the top of the column. Use the formal written method.

Example

148 ÷ 4

```
      H   T   O
          3   7
    ┌─────────────
  4 │ 1   4  ²8
```

Challenge 3

Find and complete the multiplication calculations below that match your eight division calculations in Challenges 2, 3.

37 × 4 = 148   32 × 9   29 × 4   39 × 7
24 × 7   24 × 9   33 × 4   19 × 9
29 × 6   35 × 7   23 × 6   34 × 6

44

Unit 12, Week 2, Lesson 2

Division using the formal written method (2)

Use the formal written method to calculate HTO ÷ O

Challenge 1

Sort the cards into multiples of 3, 8, 9 and 12.
You can use the same multiple more than once.

| 6 | 18 | 27 | 24 | 30 | 16 | 56 | 32 | 54 | 36 | 72 | 144 | 108 | 60 |

Challenges 2, 3

1. New resources have arrived in school and need to be divided between the numbers of classes shown. What is the approximate number each class will receive?

> **Example**
> $462 ÷ 6 \rightarrow 480 ÷ 6 = 80$

paper clips 462	pencils 288	tacks 528	butterfly clips 396	little sharpeners 315
Share between	Share between	Share between	Share between	Share between
6 classes	6 classes	6 classes	4 classes	5 classes
3 classes	8 classes	8 classes	9 classes	7 classes
7 classes	3 classes	4 classes	6 classes	3 classes

2. Choose three resources from above. Share the resources between the classes to find out exactly how many they would receive of each. Use the formal written method.

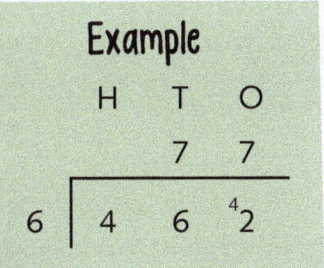

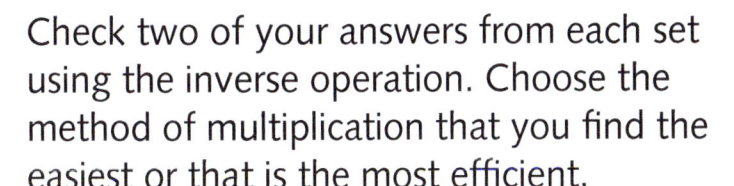

> **Example**
> ```
>     H  T  O
>        7  7
>   6 | 4  6  ⁴2
> ```

Challenge 3

Check two of your answers from each set using the inverse operation. Choose the method of multiplication that you find the easiest or that is the most efficient.

Unit 12, Week 2, Lesson 3

Division using the most efficient method

Use the most efficient method to calculate HTO ÷ O

Challenge 1

Look at each of these number sentences.
Use the symbols <, = or > to make each statement true.

a 45 ÷ 9   36 ÷ 4   b 44 ÷ 11   32 ÷ 8   c 72 ÷ 8   54 ÷ 6
d 48 ÷ 1   16 ÷ 2   e 56 ÷ 8   24 ÷ 4   f 63 ÷ 9   24 ÷ 3
g 28 ÷ 7   28 ÷ 4   h 560 ÷ 10 7 × 8   i 48 ÷ 4   9 × 1

Challenges 2, 3

Sort these calculations into two groups: those you would work out mentally and those where you would use a written method. Then work out the answer to each calculation using the most efficient method. For the calculations that need a written method, use the formal written method and remember to estimate the answer first.

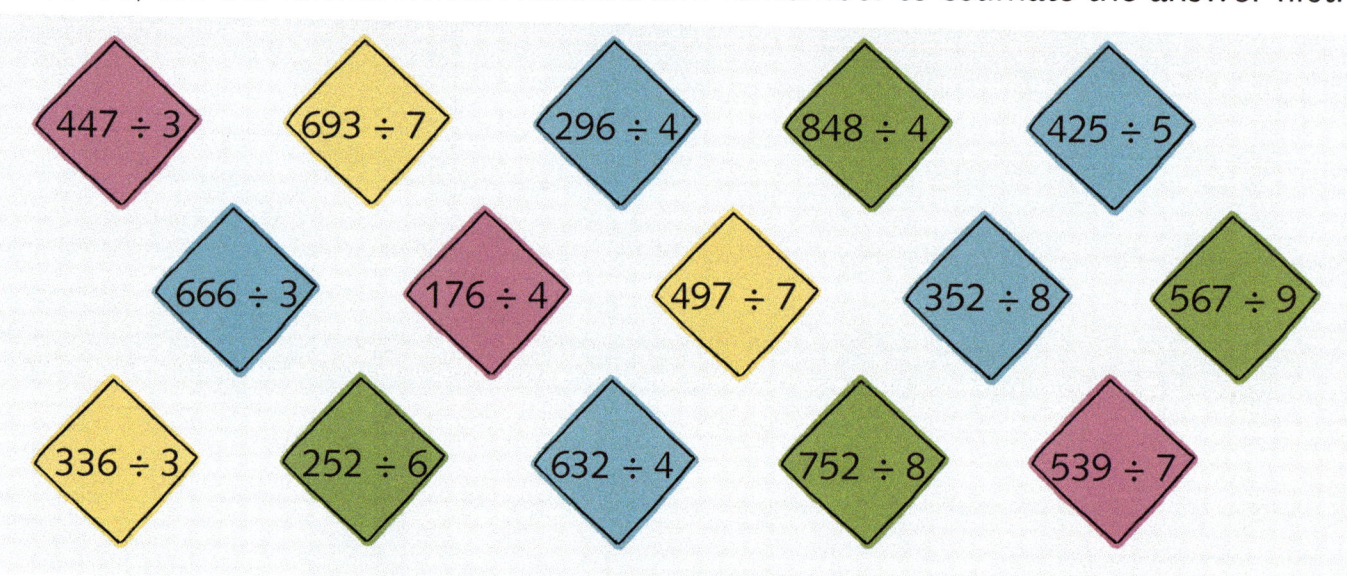

447 ÷ 3   693 ÷ 7   296 ÷ 4   848 ÷ 4   425 ÷ 5

666 ÷ 3   176 ÷ 4   497 ÷ 7   352 ÷ 8   567 ÷ 9

336 ÷ 3   252 ÷ 6   632 ÷ 4   752 ÷ 8   539 ÷ 7

Challenge 3

Choose three of your calculations from Challenges 2, 3. Write a word problem using the ideas in the boxes below.

Unit 12, Week 2, Lesson 4

Solving word problems (4)

Solve problems and reason mathematically

Challenge 1

Some of the factors are incorrect. Find the correct factors of each number and write them down.

a 30 2, 3, 7, 4, 6, 10   b 45 3, 5, 6, 8, 9, 11   c 48 3, 4, 6, 7, 8, 12

d 20 2, 4, 6, 5, 3, 10   e 18 5, 3, 4, 6, 9, 8   f 36 3, 7, 5, 10, 12, 9

Challenge 2

a The cook makes 582 sandwiches. She packs them into 6 boxes. How many sandwiches are there in each box?

b One third of the 582 sandwiches are tuna. How many sandwiches is this?

c How many sandwiches are not tuna?

d 9 classes go on the picnic. There are 243 cartons of fruit juice to share. How many cartons is this per class?

e There are 243 children at the school picnic. Each child eats 3 pieces of fruit. How many pieces of fruit did the children eat altogether?

f There are 469 apples altogether. They are placed into 7 baskets. How many apples are there in each basket?

g Ice creams cost €2 each. How much does it cost for 243 children to have one ice cream each?

h The 243 cartons of juice come in 3 different flavours. How many cartons of each flavour are there?

i There are 729 pieces of fruit altogether. If there are 469 apples, how many other fruits are there?

Challenge 3

Write your own word problems for these calculations. Swap them with a friend to solve.

a 268 × 4   b 465 ÷ 5   c 672 ÷ 8   d 354 × 6   e 300 − 72

Unit 12, Week 3, Lesson 1

Dice bar charts

Interpret and present discrete data using scaled bar charts

You will need:
- 1 cm squared paper
- ruler

Challenge 1

Keira used a dice labelled 1, 2, 2, 3, 3, 4.

The chart shows the tally marks for the numbers Keira rolled with her 1–4 dice.

1. Copy and complete the tally chart.

Numbers rolled with a 1–4 dice		
Number rolled	Tally	Frequency
1	‖‖‖ I	
2	‖‖‖ ‖‖‖ II	
3	‖‖‖ ‖‖‖ III	
4	‖‖‖ IIII	

2. Copy and complete the bar chart to show Keira's results.

3. Which number was rolled:
   a. the most?
   b. the least?

4. How many more times did Keira:
   a. roll a 2 than a 4?
   b. roll a 3 than a 1?

5. How many times did she roll the dice altogether?

Numbers rolled with a 1–4 dice

(Bar chart grid: y-axis "Number of rolls" from 0 to 14, x-axis "Number rolled" 1 to 4)

Work with a partner.

- Copy the tally chart.
- One player rolls the dice 40 times.
- The other player records each number rolled using a tally mark.

You will need:
- dice labelled 1, 2, 2, 3, 3, 4
- 1 cm squared paper
- ruler

or
- Bar Charter tool

1. Complete the frequency column in the chart.

2. Which number was rolled:
   a. the most?
   b. the least?

3. Draw a bar chart of the data from the tally chart using the Bar Charter tool or squared paper and a ruler.

4. How many times did you:
   a. roll a 2?
   b. roll an odd number?
   c. roll an even number?

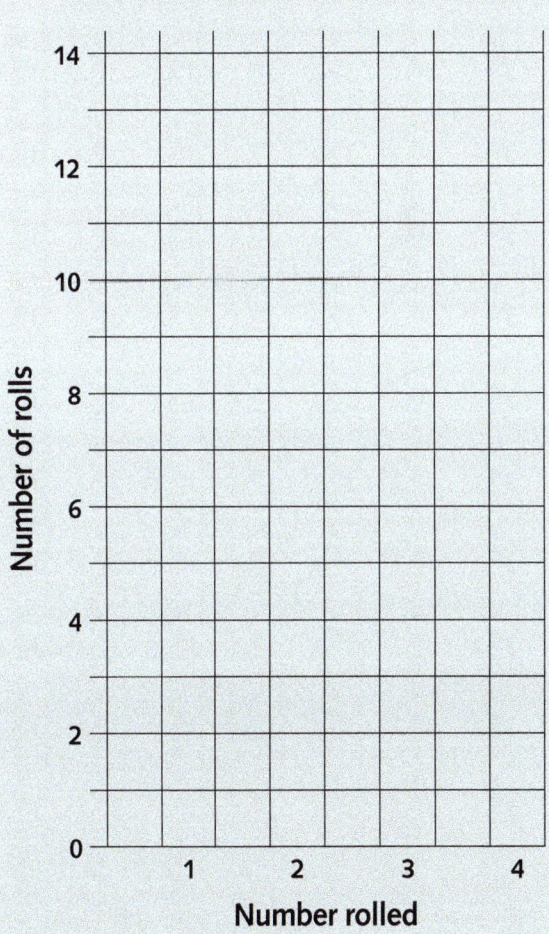

Numbers rolled with a 1–4 dice		
Number rolled	Tally	Frequency
1		
2		
3		
4		

Numbers rolled with a 1–4 dice

Work with a partner.

You will need:
- 1–6 dice

1. Keira said, "If you roll a 1–6 dice 40 times you will not roll as many 2s as you did in Challenges 2,3." Is Keira correct? Investigate.

2. Roll 40 numbers with the 1–6 dice and draw a tally chart to record the numbers you roll.

3. Compare the completed tally charts for Challenges 2,3 and Challenge 3 and write what you notice.

Unit 12, Week 3, Lesson 2

Harbour times

Interpret and present continuous data in simple time graphs

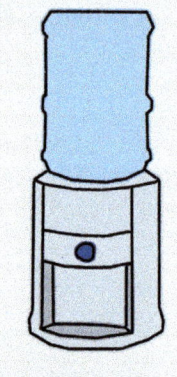

Challenge 1

There is a water dispenser in the Harbour Master's office. The table shows how many litres of water it held at hourly intervals.

1 Copy and complete the time graph using the data in the table.

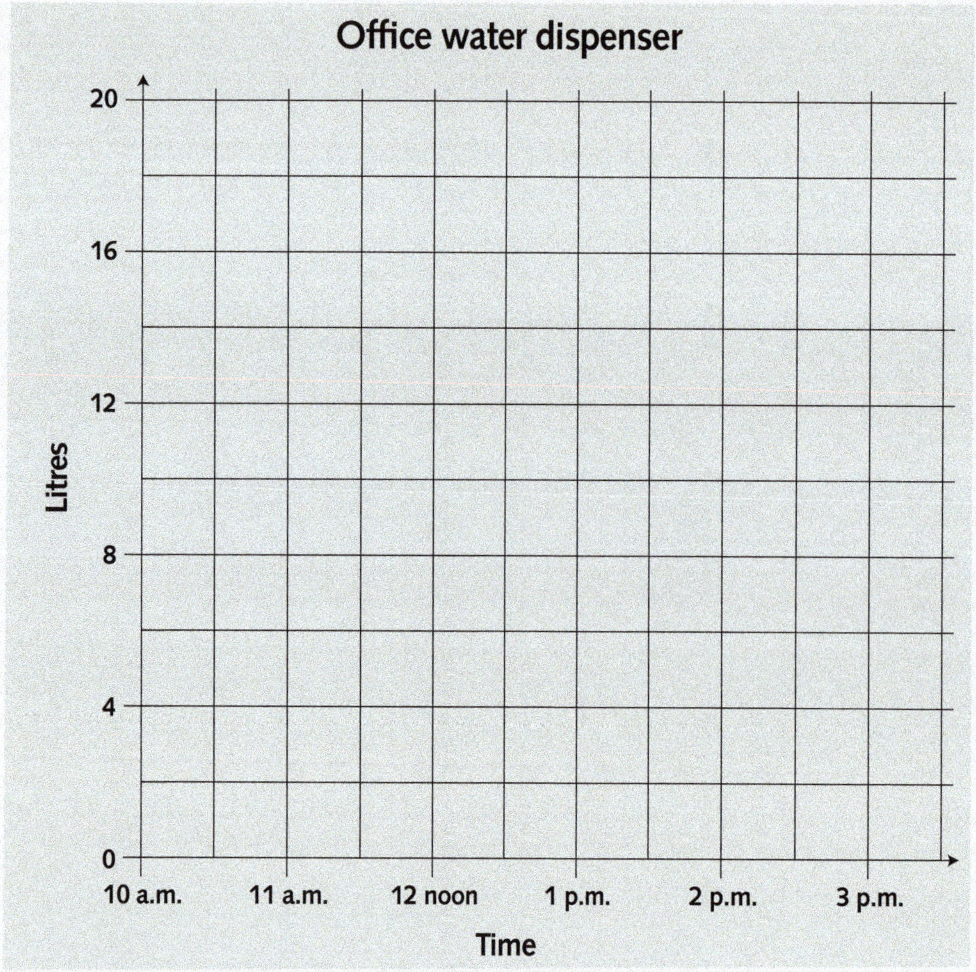

Office water dispenser

Time	Litres
10 a.m.	20
11 a.m.	18
12 noon	15
1 p.m.	11
2 p.m.	6
3 p.m.	4

You will need:
- 1 cm squared paper
- ruler

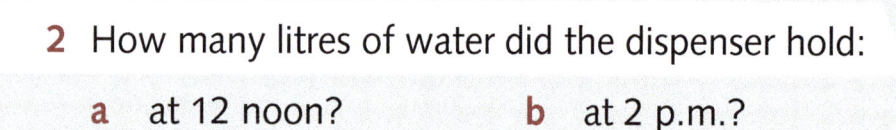

2 How many litres of water did the dispenser hold:

   a   at 12 noon?　　　　b   at 2 p.m.?

3 How many litres of water were used:

   a   before 12 noon?　　b   after 12 noon?

4 Estimate how many litres of water there were at 2:30 p.m.

Challenge 2

The table shows the depth of water in metres in the harbour at the start of each hour.

1. Copy and complete the time graph using the data in the table.

2. What was the depth of water at 7 p.m.?

3. How much deeper was the water at 9 p.m.:

   a than at 6 p.m.?

   b than at 11 p.m.?

4. Estimate the depth of water at:

   a 6:30 p.m.

   b 10:30 p.m.

Time	Depth (m)
6 p.m.	2
7 p.m.	6
8 p.m.	8
9 p.m.	10
10 p.m.	9
11 p.m.	7

You will need:
- 1 cm squared paper
- ruler

Depth of water in harbour

Challenge 3

The table shows half-hourly readings of the diesel in the tank of a fishing boat.

1. After what time did the fishing boat slow down to take on board its catch of fish?

2. How many litres of diesel were used:

   a from 9:00 p.m. to 10:30 p.m.?

   b from 9 o'clock to midnight?

3. Use the Line Grapher tool or squared paper and a ruler to draw a time graph for the data in the table.

Time	Diesel (l)
9:00 p.m.	100
9:30 p.m.	94
10:00 p.m.	88
10:30 p.m.	82
11:00 p.m.	81
11:30 p.m.	76
12:00 midnight	69

You will need:
- 1 cm squared paper
- ruler

or

- Line Grapher tool

Unit 12, Week 3, Lesson 3

Activity Centre data

Solve problems using data presented in scaled pictograms, bar charts and tables

Challenge 1

Children in Year 4 of Hill Street School spent five days at Lakeside Activity Centre at the end of May.

The pictogram shows their favourite activities.

Favourite activities at Lakeside

Archery	☺ ☺ ☺
Assault course	☺ ☺ ☺ ☺ ☺ ☺ ☺
Canoeing	☺ ☺ ☺ ☺ ☺
Rock climbing	☺ ☺ ☺ ☺
Water sports	☺ ☺ ☺ ☺
Zip wire	☺ ☺ ☺ ☺ ☺ ☺

Key
☺ 2 children

1 Which activity was:

   a the most popular?   b the least popular?

2 How many children said that their favourite activity was:

   a Zip wire?   b Archery?   c Rock climbing?

3 How many more children chose zip wire than:

   a Archery?   b Rock climbing?

4 Which activity was chosen by 12 children?

5 How many children from Hill Street School went to the Lakeside Activity Centre?

Challenge 2

At the beginning of June, children in Year 4 of Craigton School went to Lakeside Activity Centre for five days.

The bar chart shows their favourite activities.

Favourite activities at Lakeside

1. Which activity was the most popular?

2. How many more children chose Assault course as their favourite activity than:

    a   Archery?

    b   Rock climbing?

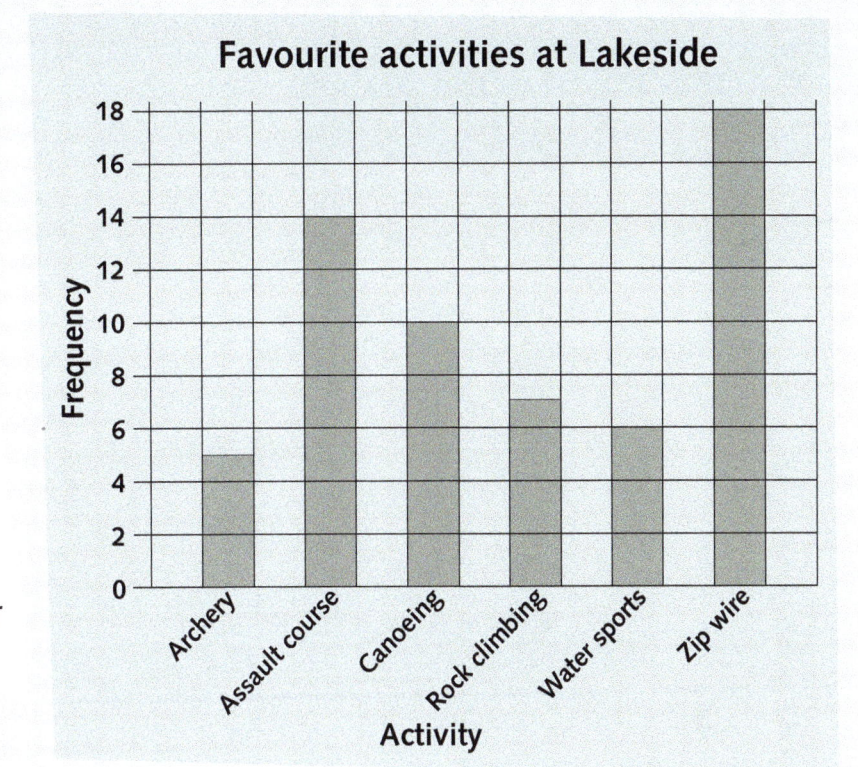

3. How many fewer children chose archery than:

    a   Canoeing?   b   Water sports?

4. Which activity had:

    a   8 fewer choices than Assault course?

    b   13 more choices than Archery?

5. Which activities were chosen by 10 or more children?

6. How many children from Craigton School went to the Lakeside Activity Centre?

Challenge 3

1. Draw two tables to show the activities chosen by Hill Street School and Craigton School.

2. What were the top two favourite activities for each school?

3. Which school had:

    a   more children who chose Canoeing and Water sports?

    b   more children who chose Rock climbing and Zip wire?

Unit 12, Week 3, Lesson 4

Travel time graphs

Solve problems using data presented in simple time graphs

Challenge 1

David delivers groceries for his online customers. The time graph shows his journey.

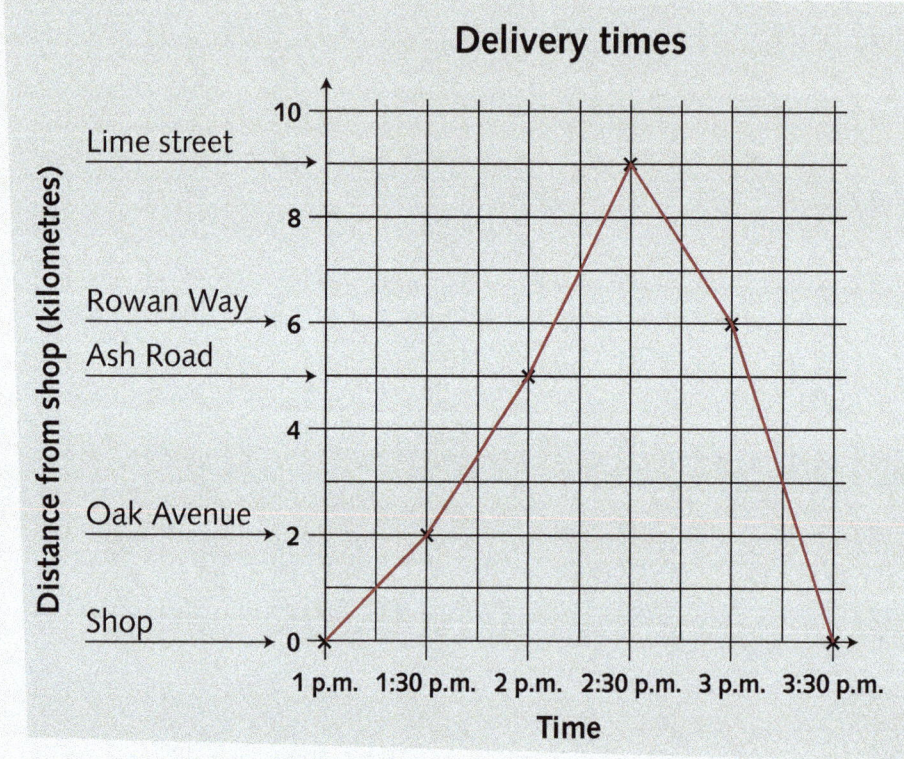

Delivery times

(Graph: Distance from shop (kilometres) vs Time from 1 p.m. to 3:30 p.m. Markers: Shop at 0, Oak Avenue at 2, Ash Road at 5, Rowan Way at 6, Lime street at 9.)

1 a Where did David deliver his first order?

   b At what time was this?

2 When did he make a delivery to:

   a Lime Street?   b Rowan Way?

3 To which address did he deliver the groceries at 2 p.m.?

4 a How far is it from the shop to Ash Road?

   b How far is it from Rowan Way to the shop?

5 About how many kilometres from the shop was David at 3:15 p.m.?

54

Nicola's family is on holiday in Scotland.

The time graph shows how they spent one of their days.

1   The family reached the fish farm at 9:30 a.m.

   a   How far had they driven from the hotel?

   b   How long did they spend there?

2   Write the time when they reached:

   a   the castle

   b   the safari park

3   How far is the safari park from:

   a   the fish farm?

   b   the hotel?

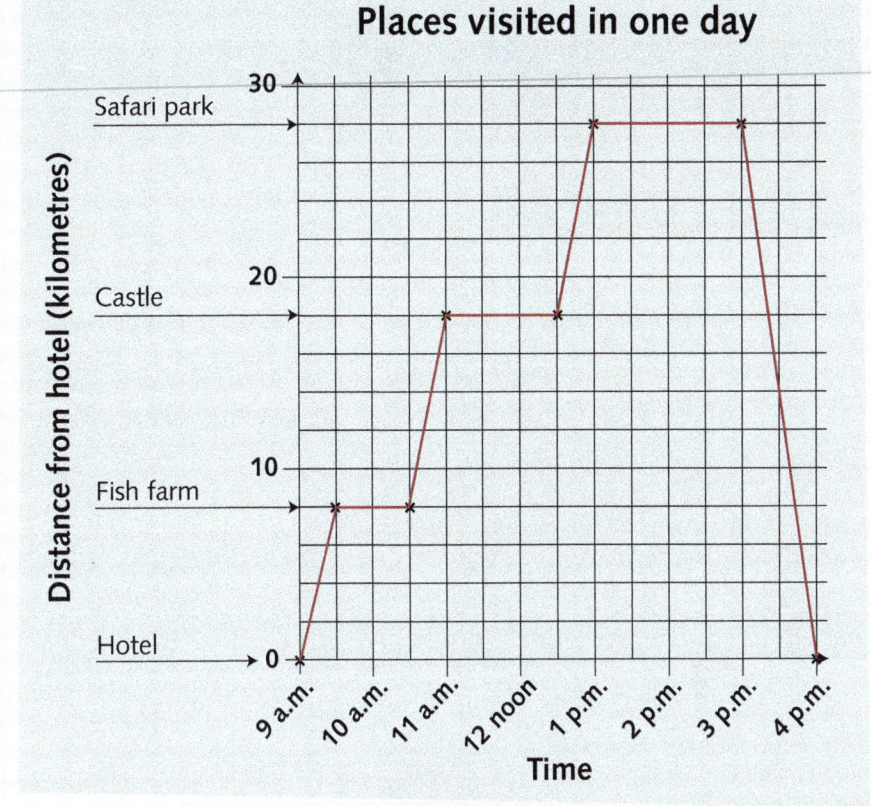

4   How many minutes longer was their stay at the safari park than at the castle?

5   How long did it take to drive from the safari park back to the hotel?

6   About how many kilometres from the hotel were they at 3:30 p.m.?

7   How many hours altogether were spent on visits to the fish farm, the castle and the safari park?

Places visited in one day

Using the Line Grapher tool or squared paper and a ruler, draw a graph which shows that the family visited the safari park in the morning and the castle and fish farm in the afternoon.

You will need:
- 1 cm squared paper
- ruler

or

- Line Grapher tool

Maths facts

Problem solving

The seven steps to solving word problems

1 Read the problem carefully.   2 What do you have to find?   3 What facts are given?
4 Which of the facts do you need?   5 Make a plan.
6 Carry out your plan to obtain your answer.   7 Check your answer.

Number and place value

1000	2000	3000	4000	5000	6000	7000	8000	9000
100	200	300	400	500	600	700	800	900
10	20	30	40	50	60	70	80	90
1	2	3	4	5	6	7	8	9
0·1	0·2	0·3	0·4	0·5	0·6	0·7	0·8	0·9
0·01	0·02	0·03	0·04	0·05	0·06	0·07	0·08	0·09

Positive and negative numbers

-10 -9 -8 -7 -6 -5 -4 -3 -2 -1 0 1 2 3 4 5 6 7 8 9 10

Addition and subtraction

Number facts

+	0	1	2	3	4	5	6	7	8	9	10
0	0	1	2	3	4	5	6	7	8	9	10
1	1	2	3	4	5	6	7	8	9	10	11
2	2	3	4	5	6	7	8	9	10	11	12
3	3	4	5	6	7	8	9	10	11	12	13
4	4	5	6	7	8	9	10	11	12	13	14
5	5	6	7	8	9	10	11	12	13	14	15
6	6	7	8	9	10	11	12	13	14	15	16
7	7	8	9	10	11	12	13	14	15	16	17
8	8	9	10	11	12	13	14	15	16	17	18
9	9	10	11	12	13	14	15	16	17	18	19
10	10	11	12	13	14	15	16	17	18	19	20

+	11	12	13	14	15	16	17	18	19	20
0	11	12	13	14	15	16	17	18	19	20
1	12	13	14	15	16	17	18	19	20	
2	13	14	15	16	17	18	19	20		
3	14	15	16	17	18	19	20			
4	15	16	17	18	19	20				
5	16	17	18	19	20					
6	17	18	19	20						
7	18	19	20							
8	19	20								
9	20									

+	0	10	20	30	40	50	60	70	80	90	100
0	0	10	20	30	40	50	60	70	80	90	100
10	10	20	30	40	50	60	70	80	90	100	110
20	20	30	40	50	60	70	80	90	100	110	120
30	30	40	50	60	70	80	90	100	110	120	130
40	40	50	60	70	80	90	100	110	120	130	140
50	50	60	70	80	90	100	110	120	130	140	150
60	60	70	80	90	100	110	120	130	140	150	160
70	70	80	90	100	110	120	130	140	150	160	170
80	80	90	100	110	120	130	140	150	160	170	180
90	90	100	110	120	130	140	150	160	170	180	190
100	100	110	120	130	140	150	160	170	180	190	200

+	110	120	130	140	150	160	170	180	190	200
0	110	120	130	140	150	160	170	180	190	200
10	120	130	140	150	160	170	180	190	200	210
20	130	140	150	160	170	180	190	200	210	220
30	140	150	160	170	180	190	200	210	220	230
40	150	160	170	180	190	200	210	220	230	240
50	160	170	180	190	200	210	220	230	240	250
60	170	180	190	200	210	220	230	240	250	260
70	180	190	200	210	220	230	240	250	260	270
80	190	200	210	220	230	240	250	260	270	280
90	200	210	220	230	240	250	260	270	280	290
100	210	220	230	240	250	260	270	280	290	300

Written methods – addition

Example: 2456 + 5378

```
  2 4 5 6
+ 5 3 7 8
---------
  7 8 3 4
      1 1
```

Written methods – subtraction

Example: 6418 – 2546

```
   5 13 11
   6 4 1 8
 - 2 5 4 6
---------
   3 8 7 2
```

Multiplication and division

Number facts

×	2	3	4	5	6	7	8	9	10	11	12
1	2	3	4	5	6	7	8	9	10	11	12
2	4	6	8	10	12	14	16	18	20	22	24
3	6	9	12	15	18	21	24	27	30	33	36
4	8	12	16	20	24	28	32	36	40	44	48
5	10	15	20	25	30	35	40	45	50	55	60
6	12	18	24	30	36	42	48	54	60	66	72
7	14	21	28	35	42	49	56	63	70	77	84
8	16	24	32	40	48	56	64	72	80	88	96
9	18	27	36	45	54	63	72	81	90	99	108
10	20	30	40	50	60	70	80	90	100	110	120
11	22	33	44	55	66	77	88	99	110	121	132
12	24	36	48	60	72	84	96	108	120	132	144

Written methods – multiplication

Example: 356 × 7

Partitioning

$356 \times 7 = (300 \times 7) + (50 \times 7) + (6 \times 7)$
$\quad\quad\quad = 2100 + 350 + 42$
$\quad\quad\quad = 2492$

Grid method

×	300	50	6
7	2100	350	42

= 2492

Expanded written method

```
    3 5 6
  ×     7
---------
     4 2   ( 6 × 7)
   3 5 0   ( 50 × 7)
 2 1 0 0   ( 300 × 7)
---------
 2 4 9 2
```

Formal written method

```
    3 5 6
  × ₃₄ 7
---------
  2 4 9 2
```

Written methods – division

Example: 486 ÷ 9

Partitioning

$486 \div 9 = (450 \div 9) + (36 \div 9)$
$\quad\quad\quad = 50 + 4$
$\quad\quad\quad = 54$

Formal written method

```
     5 4
9 ) 4 8 ³6
```

Expanded written method

```
       5 4
9 ) 4 8 6
    4 5 0   | 50 × 9
    -----
      3 6
      3 6   | 4 × 9
      ---
        0
```

57

Fractions and decimals

$\frac{1}{100} = 0.01$

$\frac{2}{100} = \frac{1}{50} = 0.02$

$\frac{5}{100} = \frac{1}{20} = 0.05$

$\frac{10}{100} = \frac{1}{10} = 0.1$

$\frac{20}{100} = \frac{1}{5} = 0.2$

$\frac{25}{100} = \frac{1}{4} = 0.25$

$\frac{50}{100} = \frac{1}{2} = 0.5$

$\frac{75}{100} = \frac{3}{4} = 0.75$

$\frac{100}{100} = 1$

Measurement

Length
1 kilometre (km) = 1000 metres (m)
0·1 km = 100 m
1 m = 100 centimetres (cm) = 1000 millimetres (mm)
0·1 m = 10 cm = 100 mm
1 cm = 10 mm
0·1 cm = 1 mm

Mass
1 kilogram (kg) = 1000 grams (g)
0·1 kg = 100 g
0·01 kg = 10 g

Capacity
1 litre (l) = 1000 millilitres (ml)
0·1 l = 100 ml
0·01 l = 10 ml

Time
1 year = 12 months
= 365 days
= 366 days (leap year)
1 week = 7 days
1 day = 24 hours
1 hour = 60 minutes
1 minute = 60 seconds

12-hour clock

24-hour clock

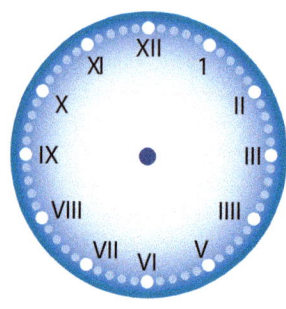

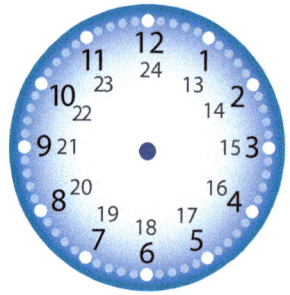

30 days has September, April, June and November. All the rest have 31, except February alone which has 28 days clear and 29 in each leap year.

Properties of shape

2-D shapes

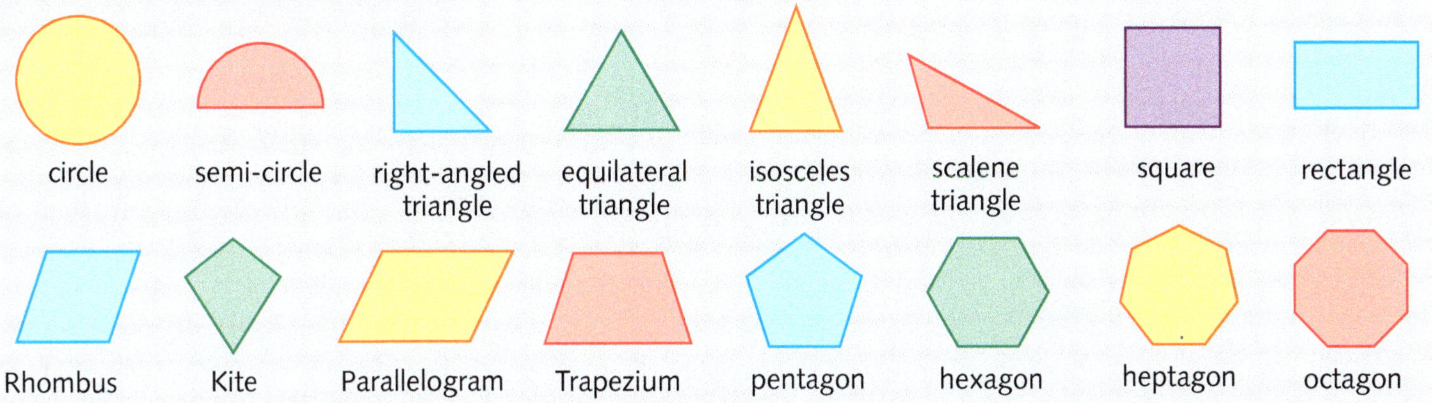

circle · semi-circle · right-angled triangle · equilateral triangle · isosceles triangle · scalene triangle · square · rectangle

Rhombus · Kite · Parallelogram · Trapezium · pentagon · hexagon · heptagon · octagon

3-D shapes

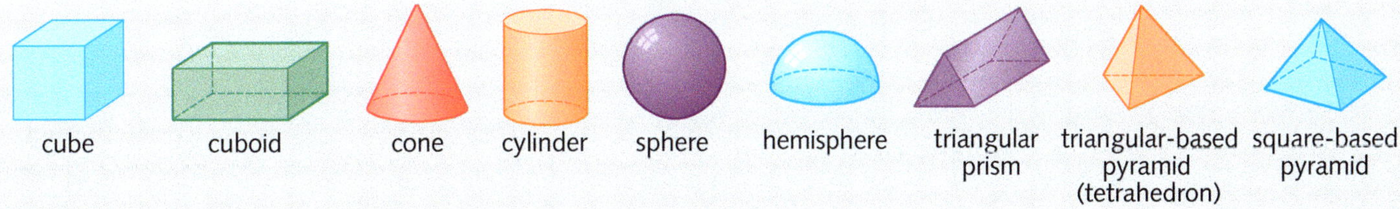

cube · cuboid · cone · cylinder · sphere · hemisphere · triangular prism · triangular-based pyramid (tetrahedron) · square-based pyramid

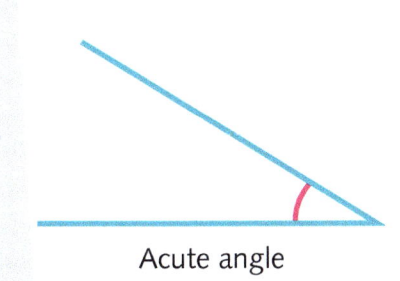

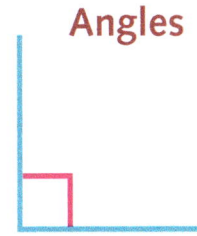

Angles

Acute angle · Right angle · Obtuse angle

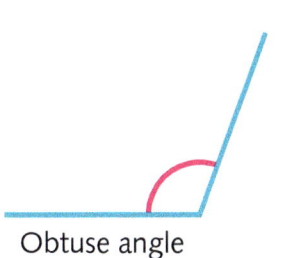

Position and direction

Coordinates

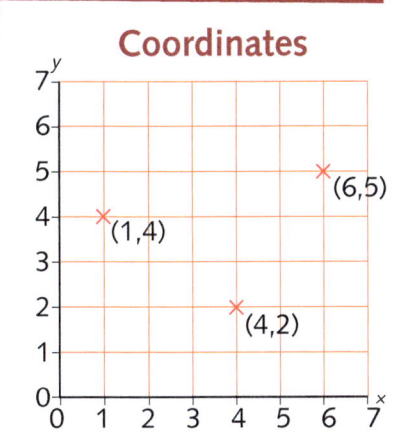

(1,4), (6,5), (4,2)

Translation

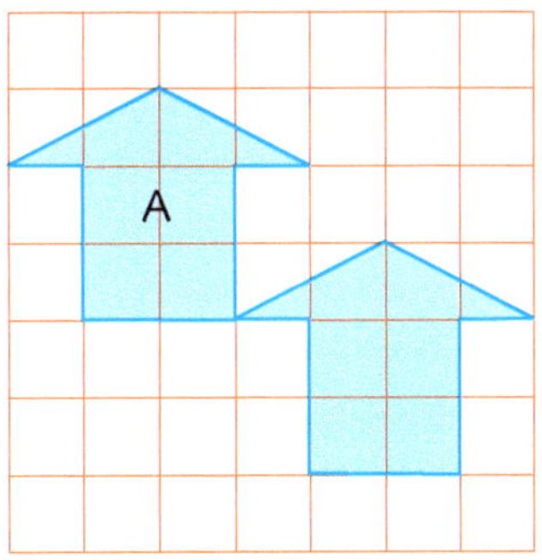

Shape A has been translated 3 squares to the right and 2 squares down.

Reflection

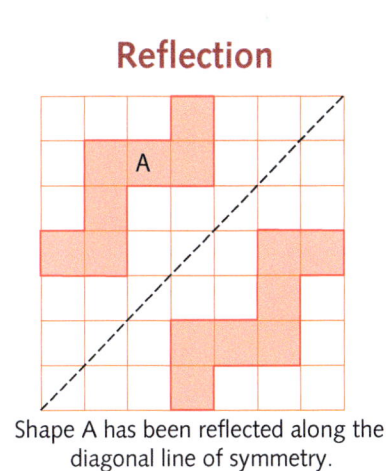

Shape A has been reflected along the diagonal line of symmetry.

William Collins' dream of knowledge for all began with the publication of his first book in 1819. A self-educated mill worker, he not only enriched millions of lives, but also founded a flourishing publishing house. Today, staying true to this spirit, Collins books are packed with inspiration, innovation and practical expertise. They place you at the centre of a world of possibility and give you exactly what you need to explore it.

Collins. Freedom to teach.

Published by Collins
An imprint of HarperCollins*Publishers*
The News Building
1 London Bridge Street
London
SE1 9GF

Browse the complete Collins catalogue at
www.collins.co.uk

© HarperCollins*Publishers* Limited 2015

10 9 8 7 6 5 4 3 2

ISBN 978-0-00-815748-7

The authors assert their moral rights to be identified as the authors of this work

All rights reserved. No part of this publication may be reproduced, stored in a retrieval system, or transmitted in any form or by any means, electronic, mechanical, photocopying, recording or otherwise, without the prior written permission of the Publisher or a licence permitting restricted copying in the United Kingdom issued by the Copyright Licensing Agency Ltd., 90 Tottenham Court Road, London W1T 4LP.

British Library Cataloguing in Publication Data
A Catalogue record for this publication is available from the British Library

Edited by Catherine Dakin, Donna Cole and Jean Rustean
Cover design and artwork by Amparo Barrera
Internal design concept by Amparo Barrera
Designed by GreenGate Publishing Services, Tonbridge, Kent
Illustrations by Louise Forshaw, Steven Woods, Gwyneth Williamson and Eva Sassin
European edition edited by: Ros and Chris Davies

Printed and bound by CPI Group (UK) Ltd, Croydon, CR0 4YY